Dawn of
Remembered
Spring

Books by Jesse Stuart

MAN WITH A BULL-TONGUE PLOW
HEAD O' W-HOLLOW
BEYOND DARK HILLS
TREES OF HEAVEN
MEN OF THE MOUNTAINS
TAPS FOR PRIVATE TUSSIE
MONGREL METTLE
ALBUM OF DESTINY
FORETASTE OF GLORY
TALES FROM THE PLUM GROVE HILLS
THE THREAD THAT RUNS SO TRUE
HIE TO THE HUNTERS
CLEARING IN THE SKY
KENTUCKY IS MY LAND
THE GOOD SPIRIT OF LAUREL RIDGE
THE YEAR OF MY REBIRTH
PLOWSHARE IN HEAVEN
GOD'S ODDLING
HOLD APRIL
A JESSE STUART READER
SAVE EVERY LAMB
DAUGHTER OF THE LEGEND
MY LAND HAS A VOICE
MR. GALLION'S SCHOOL
COME GENTLE SPRING
COME BACK TO THE FARM

For Boys and Girls

PENNY'S WORTH OF CHARACTER
THE BEATINEST BOY
RED MULE
THE RIGHTFUL OWNER
ANDY FINDS A WAY
OLD BEN

JESSE STUART

Dawn of
Remembered
Spring

McGraw-Hill Book Company
New York • St. Louis • San Francisco
Düsseldorf • Mexico • Toronto

Stuart, Jesse, date
Dawn of remembered spring.

Short stories and poems.
I. Title.
PS3537.T92516A6   1972   813'.5'2   75-37150
ISBN 0-07-062240-X

"Dawn of Remembered Spring" first appeared in *Harper's Bazaar* in the June, 1942, issue. "Old Ben" appeared in *Frontiers* Magazine, published by the Academy of Natural Sciences of Philadelphia. "The Old Are Valiant" was first published in *Mountain Life and Work*, © 1962. "Grandpa Birdwell's Last Battle" is reprinted by permission of *Esquire Magazine* © 1961 (renewed 1969). "Yoked for Life" was originally published in *The University of Kansas City Review (The University Review)*. "Love" appeared in *Story*, May–June, 1940. "Disputing Warriors" was first published in *American Forests*, April, 1957. "Time of the Cottonmouth Winds" is reprinted by permission of *Kansas Magazine (Kansas Quarterly)*. "The Usurper of Beauty Ridge" was originally published by the Indiana Council of Teachers of English in *Seven by Jesse*," © 1970. "The Blacksnake's Operation" originally appeared in *Junior Scholastic*, © 1956 by Scholastic Magazines, Inc. A somewhat different version of "Old Jackson Was My Teacher" was published in December, 1969, by the College of Education, the Ohio State University, in *Theory into Practice*, Vol. VIII, No. 5. "Bull Blacksnake Defends His Race" was first published under the title "Defense of Serpent" in *Esquire Magazine*, © 1940 by Esquire, Inc. "A Thousand Years Is a Long Time" is reprinted by permission of *The Arizona Quarterly*, where it appeared in the Autumn, 1967, issue.

This is to her from one
who has observed,
protected, and recorded
"You living things that crawl
and run and fly."

Contents

· Contents ·

Stories

I

Dawn of Remembered Spring

◄§|| "Be careful, Shan," Mom said. "I'm afraid if you wade that creek that a water moccasin will bite you."

"All right, Mom."

"You know what happened to Roy Deer last Sunday!"

"Yes, Mom!"

"He's nigh at the point of death," she said. "I'm going over there now to see him. His leg's swelled hard as a rock and it's turned black as black-oak bark. They're not looking for Roy to live until midnight tonight."

"All water moccasins ought to be killed, hadn't they, Mom?"

"Yes, they're pizen things, but you can't kill them," Mom said. "They're in all these creeks around here. There's so many of them we can't kill 'em all."

Mom stood at the foot-log that crossed the creek in front of our house. Her white apron was starched stiff; I heard it rustle when Mom put her hand in the little pocket in the right upper corner to get tobacco crumbs for her pipe. Mom wore her slat bonnet that shaded her sun-tanned face—a bonnet with strings that came under her chin and tied in a bowknot.

"I feel uneasy," Mom said as she filled her long-stemmed clay-stone pipe with bright burley crumbs, tamped them down with her index finger, and struck a match on the rough bark of an apple tree that grew on the creek bank by the foot-log.

"Don't feel uneasy about me," I said.

"But I do," Mom said. "Your Pa out groundhog huntin' and I'll be away at Deer's—nobody at home but you, and so many pizen snakes around this house."

Mom blew a cloud of blue smoke from her pipe. She walked across the foot-log, her long clean dress sweeping the weed stubble where Pa had mown the weeds along the path with a scythe so we could leave the house without getting our legs wet by the dew-covered weeds.

When Mom walked out of sight around the turn of the pasture hill and the trail of smoke that she left behind her had disappeared into the light blue April air, I crossed the garden fence at the wild-plum thicket.

Everybody gone, I thought. I am left alone. I'll do as I please. A water moccasin bit Roy Deer but a water moccasin will never bite me. I'll get me a club from this wild-plum thicket and I'll wade up the creek killing water moccasins.

There was a dead wild-plum sprout standing among the thicket of living sprouts. It was about the size of a tobacco stick. I stepped out of my path into the wild-plum thicket. Barefooted, I walked among the wild-plum thorns. I uprooted the dead wild-plum sprout. There was a bulge on it where roots had once been; now the roots had rotted in the earth. It was like a maul with this big bulge on the end of it. It would be good to hit water moccasins with.

The mules played in the pasture. It was Sunday, their day of rest. And the mules knew it. This was Sunday and it was my day of rest. It was my one day of freedom, too,

[4]

when Mom and Pa were gone and I was left alone. I would like to be a man now, I thought; I'd love to plow the mules, run a farm, and kill snakes. A water moccasin bit Roy Deer but one would never bite me.

The bright sunlight of April played over the green Kentucky hills. Sunlight fell onto the creek of blue water that twisted like a crawling snake around the high bluffs and between the high rocks. In many places, dwarf willows, horseweeds, ironweeds, and wild grapevines shut away the sunlight, and the creek waters stood in quiet cool puddles. These little puddles under the shade of weeds, vines, and willows were the places where the water moccasins lived.

I rolled my overall legs above my knees so I wouldn't wet them and Mom wouldn't know I'd been wading the creek. I started wading up the creek toward the head of the Hollow. I carried my wild-plum club across my shoulder, with both hands gripped tightly around the small end of it. I was ready to maul the first water moccasin I saw.

"One of you old water moccasins bit Roy Deer," I said bravely, clinching my grip tighter around my club, "but you won't bite me."

As I waded the cool creek waters, my bare feet touched gravel on the creek bottom. When I touched a water-soaked stick on the bottom of the creek bed, I'd think it was a snake and I'd jump. I'd wade into banks of quicksand. I'd sink into the sand above my knees. It was hard to pull my legs out of this quicksand and when I pulled them out they'd be covered with thin quicky mud that the next puddle of water would wash away.

"A water moccasin," I said to myself. I was scared to look at him. He was wrapped around a willow that was

[5]

bent over the creek. He was sleeping in the sun. I slipped toward him quietly—step by step—with my club drawn over my shoulder. Soon as I got close enough to reach him, I came over my shoulder with the club. I hit the water moccasin a powerful blow that mashed its head flat against the willow. It fell dead into the water. I picked it up by the tail and threw it upon the bank.

"One gone," I said to myself.

The water was warm around my feet and legs. The sharp-edged gravels hurt the bottoms of my feet but the soft sand soothed them. Butterflies swarmed over my head and around me—alighting on the wild pink phlox that grew in clusters along the creek bank. Wild honeybees, bumblebees, and butterflies worked on the elder blossoms, the shoemake blossoms, the beet-red finger-long blossoms of the ironweed, and the whitish pink-covered smartweed blossoms. Birds sang among the willows and flew up and down the creek with four-winged snakefeeders in their bills.

This is what I like to do, I thought. I love to kill snakes. I'm not afraid of snakes. I laughed to think how afraid of snakes Mom was—how she stuck a potato-digger tine through a big rusty-golden copperhead's skin just enough to pin him to the earth and hold him so he couldn't get under our floor. He fought the potato-digger handle until Pa came home from work and killed him. Where the snake had thrown poison over the ground, it killed the weeds, and weeds didn't grow on this spot again for four years.

Once when Mom was making my bed upstairs, she heard a noise of something running behind the paper that was pasted over the cracks between the logs; the paper split and a house snake six feet long fell onto the floor with a mouse in his mouth. Mom killed him with a bed slat. She called me once to bring her a goose-neck hoe upstairs quickly. I ran upstairs and killed two cow-snakes restin' on the wall plate. And Pa killed twenty-eight copperheads out of a two-acre oat field in the Hollow above the house one spring season.

"Snakes—snakes," Mom used to say, "are goin' to run us out'n this Hollow."

"It's because these woods haven't been burnt out in years," Pa'd always answer. "Back when I's a boy the old people burnt the woods out every spring to kill the snakes. Got so anymore there isn't enough good timber for a board tree and people have had to quit burning up the good timber. Snakes are about to take the woods again."

I thought about the snakes Pa had killed in the cornfield and the tobacco patch and how nearly copperheads had come to biting me and how I'd always seen the snake in time to cut his head off with a hoe or get out of his way. I thought of the times I had heard a rattlesnake's warning and how I'd run when I hadn't seen the snake. As I thought this—plop—a big water moccasin fell from the creek bank into a puddle of water.

"I'll get you," I said. "You can't fool me! You can't stand muddy water."

With my wild-plum club, I stirred the water until it was muddy. I waited for the water moccasin to stick his head above the water. Where wild ferns dipped down from the bank's edge and touched the water, I saw the snake's head rise slowly above the water—watchin' me with his lidless eyes. I swung sideways with my club like batting at a ball. I couldn't swing over my shoulder, for there were willow limbs above my head.

I surely got him, I thought. I waited to see. Soon something like milk spread over the water. "I got 'im." I raked in the water with my club and lifted from the bottom of the creek bed a water moccasin long as my club. It was longer than I was tall. I threw him upon the bank and moved slowly up the creek—looking on every drift, stump, log, and sunny spot. I looked for a snake's head along the edges of the creek bank where ferns dipped over and touched the water.

I waded up the creek all day killing water moccasins. If one was asleep on the bank, I slipped upon him quietly as a cat. I mauled him with the big end of my wild-plum club. I killed him in his sleep. He never knew what struck him. If a brush caught the end of my club and caused me to miss and let the snake get into a puddle of water, I muddied the water and waited for him to stick his head above the water. When he did, I got him. Not one water moccasin got away from me. It was four o'clock when I stepped from the creek onto the bank. I'd killed fifty-three water moccasins.

Water moccasins are not half as dangerous as turtles, I thought. A water moccasin can't bite you under the water, for he gets his mouth full of water. A turtle can bite you under water and when one bites you he won't let loose until it thunders, unless you cut his head off. I'd been afraid of turtles all day because I didn't have a knife in my pocket to cut one's head off if it grabbed my foot and held it.

When I left the creek, I was afraid of the snakes I'd killed. I didn't throw my club away. I gripped the club until my hands hurt. I looked below my path, above my path, and in front of me. When I saw a stick on the ground, I thought it was a snake. I eased up to it quietly as a cat trying to catch a bird. I was ready to hit it with my club.

What will Mom think when I tell her I've killed fifty-three water moccasins, I thought. A water moccasin bit Roy Deer but one's not going to bite me. I paid the snakes back for biting him. It was good enough for them. Roy wasn't bothering the water moccasin that bit him. He was just crossing the creek at the foot-log and it jumped from the grass and bit him.

Shadows lengthened from the tall trees. The Hollow was deep and the creek flowed softly in the cool recesses of evening shadows. There was one patch of sunlight. It was upon the steep broom sedge–covered bluff above the path.

"Snakes," I cried, "snakes a-fightin' and they're not water moccasins! They're copperheads!"

They were wrapped around each other. Their lidless eyes looked into each other's eyes. Their hard lips touched each other's lips. They did not move. They did not pay any attention to me. They looked at one another.

I'll kill 'em, I thought, if they don't kill one another in this fight.

I stood in the path with my club ready. I had heard snakes fought each other but I'd never seen them fight.

"What're you lookin' at, Shan?" Uncle Alf Skinner asked. He walked up the path with a cane in his hand.

"Snakes a-fightin'."

"Snakes a-fightin'?"

"Yes."

"I never saw it in my life."

"I'll kill 'em both if they don't finish the fight," I said. "I'll club 'em to death."

"Snakes a-fightin', Shan," he shouted, "you are too young

to know! It's snakes in love! Don't kill 'em—just keep your eye on 'em until I bring Martha over here! She's never seen snakes in love!"

Uncle Alf ran around the turn of the hill. He brought Aunt Martha back with him. She was carrying a basket of greens on her arm and the case knife that she'd been cutting greens with in her hand.

"See 'em, Martha," Uncle Alf said. "Look up there in that broom sedge!"

"I'll declare," she said. "I've lived all my life and I never saw this. I've wondered about snakes!"

She stood with a smile on her wrinkled lips. Uncle Alf stood with a wide smile on his deep-lined face. I looked at them and wondered why they looked at these copperheads and smiled. Uncle Alf looked at Aunt Martha. They smiled at each other.

"Shan, Shan!" I heard Mom calling.

"I'm here," I shouted.

"Where've you been?" she asked as she turned around the bend of the hill with a switch in her hand.

"Be quiet, Sal," Uncle Alf said. "Come here and look for yourself!"

"What is it?" Mom asked.

"Snakes in love," Uncle Alf said.

Mom was mad. "Shan, I feel like limbing you," she said. "I've hunted every place for you! Where've you been?"

"Killin' snakes," I answered.

"Roy Deer is dead," she said. "That's how dangerous it is to fool with snakes."

"I paid the snakes back for him," I said. "I've killed fifty-three water moccasins!"

"Look, Sal!"

"Yes, Alf, I see," Mom said.

Mom threw her switch on the ground. Her eyes were wide apart. The frown left her face.

"It's the first time I ever saw anything like this. Shan, you go tell your Pa to come and look at this."

I was glad to do anything for Mom. I was afraid of her switch. When I brought Pa back to the sunny bank where the copperheads were loving, Art and Sadie Baker were there and Tom and Ethel Riggs—and there were a lot of strangers there. They were looking at the copperheads wrapped around each other with their eyes looking into each other's eyes and their hard lips touching each other's lips.

"You hurry to the house, Shan," Pa said, "and cut your stove wood for tonight."

"I'd like to kill these copperheads," I said.

"Why?" Pa asked.

"Fightin'," I said.

Uncle Alf and Aunt Martha laughed as I walked down the path carrying my club. It was something—I didn't know what; all the crowd watching the snakes were smiling. Their faces were made over new. The snakes had done something to them. Their wrinkled faces were as bright as the spring sunlight on the bluff; their eyes were shiny as the creek was in the noonday sunlight. And they laughed and talked to one another. I heard their laughter grow fainter as I walked down the path toward the house. Their laughter was louder than the wild honeybees I had heard swarming over the shoemake, alderberry, and wild phlox blossoms along the creek.

[11]

II

Old Ben

◆§‖ One morning in July when I was walking across a clover field to a sweet-apple tree, I almost stepped on him. There he lay coiled like heavy strands of black rope. He was a big bull blacksnake. We looked at each other a minute, and then I stuck the toe of my shoe up to his mouth. He drew his head back in a friendly way. He didn't want trouble. Had he shown the least fight, I would have soon finished him. My father had always told me there was only one good snake—a dead one.

When the big fellow didn't show any fight, I reached down and picked him up by the neck. When I lifted him he was as long as I was tall. That was six feet. I started calling him Old Ben as I held him by the neck and rubbed his back. He enjoyed having his back rubbed and his head stroked. Then I lifted him into my arms. He was the first snake I'd ever been friendly with. I was afraid at first to let Old Ben wrap himself around me. I thought he might wrap himself around my neck and choke me.

The more I petted him, the more affectionate he became. He was so friendly I decided to trust him. I wrapped him around my neck a couple of times and let him loose. He crawled down one arm and went back to my neck, around and down the other arm and back again. He stuck out his forked tongue to the sound of my voice as I talked to him.

"I wouldn't kill you at all," I said. "You're a friendly snake. I'm taking you home with me."

I headed home with Old Ben wrapped around my neck and shoulders. When I started over the hill by the pine grove, I met my cousin Wayne Holbrook coming up the hill. He stopped suddenly when he saw me. He started backing down the hill.

"He's a pet, Wayne," I said. "Don't be afraid of Old Ben."

It was a minute before Wayne could tell me what he wanted. He had come to borrow a plow. He kept a safe distance as we walked on together.

Before we reached the barn, Wayne got brave enough to touch Old Ben's long body.

"What are you going to do with him?" Wayne asked. "Uncle Mick won't let you keep him!"

"Put him in the corncrib," I said. "He'll have plenty of delicate food in there. The cats we keep at this barn have grown fat and lazy on the milk we feed 'em."

I opened the corncrib door and took Old Ben from around my neck because he was beginning to get warm and a little heavy.

"This will be your home," I said. "You'd better hide under the corn."

Besides my father, I knew Old Ben would have another enemy at our home. He was our hunting dog, Blackie, who would trail a snake, same as a possum or mink. He had treed blacksnakes, and my father had shot them from the trees. I knew Blackie would find Old Ben, because he followed us to the barn each morning.

The first morning after I'd put Old Ben in the corncrib, Blackie followed us. He started toward the corncrib holding his head high, sniffing. He stuck his nose up to a crack in the crib and began to bark. Then he tried to tear a plank off.

"Stop it, Blackie," Pa scolded him. "What's the matter with you? Have you taken to barking at mice?"

"Blackie is not barking at a mouse," I said. "I put a blacksnake in there yesterday!"

"A blacksnake?" Pa asked, looking unbelievingly. "A blacksnake?"

"Yes, a pet blacksnake," I said.

"Have you gone crazy?" he said. "I'll move a thousand bushels of corn to get that snake!"

"You won't mind this one," I said. "You and Mom will love him."

My father said a few unprintable words before we started back to the house. After breakfast, when Pa and Mom came came to the barn, I was already there. I had opened the crib door and there was Old Ben. He'd crawled up front and was coiled on a sack. I put my hand down and he crawled up my arm to my neck and over my shoulder. When Mom and Pa reached the crib, I thought Pa was going to faint.

"He has a pet snake," Mom said.

"Won't be a bird or a young chicken left on this place," Pa said. "Every time I pick up an ear of corn in that crib, I'll be jumping."

"Pa, he won't hurt you," I said, patting the snake's head. "He's a natural pet, or somebody has tamed him. And he's not going to bother birds and young chickens when there are so many mice in this crib."

"Mick, let him keep the snake," Mom said. "I won't be afraid of it."

This was the beginning of a long friendship.

Mom went to the corncrib morning after morning and shelled corn for her geese and chickens. Often Old Ben would be lying in front on his burlap sack. Mom watched him at first from the corner of her eye. Later she didn't bother to watch him any more than she did a cat that came up for his milk.

Later it occurred to us that Old Ben might like milk, too. We started leaving milk for him. We never saw him drink it, but his pan was always empty when we returned. We know the mice didn't drink it, because he took care of them.

"One thing is certain," Mom said one morning when she went to shell corn. "We don't find any more corn chewed up by the mice and left on the floor."

July passed and August came. My father got used to Old Ben, but not until he had proved his worth. Ben had done something our nine cats couldn't. He had cleaned the corncrib of mice.

Then my father began to worry about Old Ben's going after water, and Blackie's finding his track. So he put water in the crib.

September came and went. We began wondering where our pet would go when days grew colder. One morning in early October we left milk for Old Ben, and it was there when we went back that afternoon. But Old Ben wasn't there.

"Old Ben's a good pet for the warm months," Pa said. "But in the winter months, my cats will have to do the work. Maybe Blackie got him!"

"He might have holed up for the winter in the hayloft," I told Pa after we had removed all the corn and didn't find him. "I'm worried about him. I've had a lot of pets—ground hogs, crows and hawks—but Old Ben's the best yet."

November, December, January, February, and March came and went. Of course we never expected to see Old Ben in one of those months. We doubted if we ever would see him again.

One day early in April I went to the corncrib, and Old Ben lay stretched across the floor. He looked taller than I was now. His skin was rough and his long body had a flabby appearance. I knew Old Ben needed mice and milk. I picked him up, petted him, and told him so. But the chill of early April was still with him. He got his tongue out slower to answer the kind words I was saying to him. He tried to crawl up my arm but he couldn't make it.

That spring and summer mice got scarce in the corncrib and Old Ben got daring. He went over to the barn and crawled up into the hayloft, where he had many feasts. But he made one mistake.

He crawled from the hayloft down into Fred's feed box, where it was cool. Old Fred was our horse.

There he lay coiled when the horse came in and put his nose down on top of Old Ben. Fred let out a big snort and started kicking. He kicked down a partition, and then turned his heels on his feed box and kicked it down. Lucky for Old Ben that he got out in one piece. But he got back to his crib.

Old Ben became a part of our barnyard family, a pet and darling of all. When children came to play with my brother and sisters, they always went to the crib and got Old Ben. He enjoyed the children, who were afraid of him at first but later learned to pet this kind old reptile.

[17]

Summer passed and the late days of September were very humid. Old Ben failed one morning to drink his milk. We knew it wasn't time for him to hole up for the winter.

We knew something had happened.

Pa and I moved the corn searching for him. Mom made a couple of trips to the barn lot to see if we had found him. But all we found was the rough skin he had shed last spring.

"Fred's never been very sociable with Old Ben since he got in his box that time," Pa said. "I wonder if he could have stomped Old Ben to death. Old Ben could've been crawling over the barn lot, and Fred saw his chance to get even!"

"We'll see," I said.

Pa and I left the crib and walked to the barn lot. He went one way and I went the other, each searching the ground.

Mom came through the gate and walked over where my father was looking. She started looking around, too.

"We think Fred might've got him," Pa said. "We're sure Fred's got it in for him over Old Ben getting in his feed box last summer."

"You're accusing Fred wrong," Mom said. "Here's Old Ben's track in the sand."

I ran over to where Mom had found the track. Pa went over to look, too.

"It's no use now," Pa said, softly. "Wouldn't have taken anything for that snake. I'll miss him on that burlap sack every morning when I come to feed the horses. Always looked up at me as if he understood."

The last trace Old Ben had left was in the corner of the lot near the hogpen. His track went straight to the woven wire fence and stopped.

"They've got him," Pa said. "Old Ben trusted everything and everybody. He went for a visit to the wrong place. He didn't last long among sixteen hogs. They go wild over a snake. Even a biting copperhead can't stop a hog. There won't be a trace of Old Ben left."

We stood silently for a minute looking at the broad, smooth track Old Ben had left in the sand.

III

The Old Are Valiant

&§|| "It's a good place for snakes out here," my father said as he stood leaning on his hoe handle. "I'm almost afraid to pull the weeds from around these potato vines. Afraid I'll put my hand down on a copperhead that's coolin' himself under a vine."

My father's breath came fast, for he had been digging hard with his hoe. Sweat popped out over his face, ran down the end of his nose, and dripped on the dusty mulch he had hilled around a potato vine.

"What do we care about snakes?" I told him. "We've got Jerry-B with us, and a snake won't have a chance. He's a young dog with good teeth and he's powerful."

Jerry-B was behind us, sniffing in the tall crab grass.

"Jerry-B's got enough grit, I reckon," my father admitted, "but he's not big enough. He won't weigh over eighteen pounds."

"Big enough to kill a snake," I said. "He's got a nose good enough to ferret all the snakes out of these weeds."

"I don't know about his smellin' a blacksnake," my father said. "But I can smell a copperhead myself. They're not hard to smell. One smells like hot cucumbers in the sun."

Jerry-B wriggled past us through the weeds. His short legs moved cautiously. He sniffed as he moved along. His salt-and-pepper–colored body was dotted with black. His half-curled hair bristled against the weeds as he snaked the potatoes for us.

We leaned on our hoe handles again and watched the dog until his short body was lost among the tall mass of weeds. We watched the weeds shake the way he had gone. Then we gripped our hoe handles and started digging again.

"We can't make much headway against this crab grass," my father said. "We've worked two days and have hoed only twenty-four rows."

We stood under a sassafras bush at the end of our rows to shade a few minutes. We wiped sweat from our smarting eyes. We looked over the clean potato rows below and the weedy rows above us on the backbone of the ridge—a potato patch surrounded by thickets of wild gooseberries and huckleberries where the hot smelly wind was smothery to breathe.

My father mopped his wrinkled brow with his sweat-soaked bandanna.

"Believe I smell some kind of a snake," he said as he began to hoe another row across the field. "It smells like sour dock."

"Look!" I shouted.

I pointed toward the snake. We took our hoes and ran toward the other end of the potato patch. Soon as we got near the big blacksnake, he stopped to look at us with eyes that gleamed like small black agates in the sun.

"I'm goin' to kill him," I said. "I'm goin' to kill him with this gooseneck hoe! He's so big I might break my hoe handle when I hit 'im!"

"Don't do it," my father said, grabbing my hoe handle.

"This snake reminds me of the snakes I used to see around this ridge when I was a young man. I could always tell when there was a snake sunnin' on a rock. My horse would rear up with me and stand on his hind feet and charge! I'd look around and see a big bull snake sunnin' on a rock in a huckleberry patch. I'd pull my .38 Special from the holster and feed him the hot lead. I've never liked a snake."

The big bull blacksnake lay with his head in one potato row, his body across two rows, and his tail in the fourth row. His body, in the largest part, was almost as large as the calf of my leg. His long body was slick as a peeled hickory tree and black as charcoal around a new-ground stump.

"That snake's long as a fence rail," I said.

"See, my nose didn't lie to me," my father told me. "I smelled that snake."

"Look, here comes Jerry-B," I said.

"He's trackin'," my father said. "Let him come up to him. See what the snake will do; I'll bet he'll put up a fight; He's an old residenter."

"Snake's almost big enough to swallow him," I sighed.

"But Jerry-B's tough," my father said. "He's been shot twice. The shots didn't kill him. He's been run over by a jolt wagon with two men in it. He got all right from that. He's a tough young dog. Now, let's see what he can do when he meets this old snake."

Jerry-B shook the tall weeds among the unhoed rows of potatoes as he tracked the snake toward our clean rows.

Jerry-B didn't look at us. He held his nose on the dry-parched earth where the blacksnake had left its broad trail across the dust. As soon as the bull blacksnake's lidless eyes saw Jerry-B sniffling the dust, he began to contract his big body from his head halfway down leaving his tail perfectly still.

"He's fought dogs before," my father said.

But Jerry-B sniffed, getting closer and closer as the bull blacksnake waited for him. Jerry-B came to the snake's tail that lay still as a wilted weed on the dusty ground. It was so still that Jerry-B Boneyard must have thought the snake was dead. He didn't look up, but his little hairy nose sniffled as he ran upon the snake's body without looking up. The big snake aimed at Jerry-B's head.

"Whow!" His powerful body shot forth with his big mouth open, and his iron lips hit Jerry-B between the eyes.

The force of the snake set Jerry-B back on his tail. He didn't whimper but jumped high in the air as the snake contracted to strike again. Jerry-B was now on his feet, and he was as made as a wet hornet.

"He's one of the old residenter snakes that's come from one of the cliffs," my father bragged. "He might be one of the snakes I used to shoot at when I was a young man! That was fifty years ago."

Before he had finished his words, the snake struck half the length of his long body at Jerry-B.

"That snake's riled." My father stepped back to give them room to fight. "He knows how to fight."

"He's big enough to swallow Jerry-B," I said again.

"If that snake swallows him, he'll have a mess hard to digest," my father said, grinning. "Jerry-B won't lay very well on the snake's stummick. He never would lay any place very long."

Jerry-B ran in to bite the snake, But its neck was too big for his small mouth to cover, and its hide was too thick and tough for his small saw-brier–sharp teeth to penetrate.

The snake contracted his body, catching Jerry-B in two coils, and throwing him back into the next potato row.

"I've never seen anything like that," my father shouted. "It's the best fight I ever saw. I'll bet you Jerry-B can't kill that old residenter."

"I won't bet," I said.

Now Jerry-B was running at the snake, making him strike. When the snake struck, Jerry-B jumped back and let him strike the wind.

"He's tryin' to wear the snake out," my father said. "But he'll never do it. Not that old residenter."

No matter how often Jerry-B made him strike at the wind, the big bull snake didn't tire. He quit striking when he saw the tactics Jerry-B was using. He contracted to a half coil, stuck out his tongue, and waited for the dog to make the next move. Now Jerry-B's tongue got thinner, and it was covered with flakes of spittle. They wet the whiskers around his mouth. Dust settled on his whiskers until there was a loblolly of mud around his mouth.

The potato vines around the snake and dog were mashed as flat against the dusty ground as dead autumn leaves weighted with snow. The leaves on the potato vines had been trampled by the dog's feet until they wilted in the blazing sun like the weeds we had cut with our hoes.

When Jerry-B learned how smart the snake was, he walked in for a rough-and-tumble fight. Before he reached him, the big blacksnake struck him on the jaw and set him back. Before he could come at the snake again, the bull blacksnake had re-coiled and struck him again and again. Jerry-B now dropped back the width of a potato row, lay flat on his stomach, and eyed the blacksnake.

"He's besiegin' the snake," my father laughed as he

[25]

leaned on his hoe handle. "He doesn't want him to escape."

There was a distant growl of thunder in the sky far over Whetstone. In the hot sky above us, a few mare's-tail dingy-white clouds lay like potato ridges against the blue.

"That's the way the rains come," my father said. "How we need rain!"

Jerry-B lay flat on the ground watching the snake while the snake watched him. He panted harder than I had ever seen him. His sides moved in and out like a bee smoker. Spittle dripped from his muddy whiskers. His long barks were reduced to short grunts. His black eyes, under the long wisps of hair that dropped over them, danced with fire. He had found something he couldn't conquer. He couldn't pick this snake up and sling it in two as he had done all the other snakes he had found.

" 'Spect we'd better get back to our work, Shan," my father sighed. "I'd like to finish this patch before the rain."

"It's awful hot. And we're leavin' a good fight."

"I know the fight's not over."

As we spoke, the bull snake must have thought it was over, for he started crawling away, over a potato ridge toward Sulphur Spring Hollow. Slowly he crawled, with his forked tongue stuck out in the hot wind. Jerry-B jumped to his feet, ran around a potato vine and bit the snake. The snake stopped, coiled for another fight, but Jerry-B fell flat on his stomach, and the snake missed him.

"It's another siege," my father said. "But the snake has gained a row. He's makin' for that thicket, and if he gets to it, Jerry-B can't handle him."

Over Whetstone Creek we could hear thunder. White thunderheads boiled upon the sky above the distant rim of the Whetstone ridges. We picked up our hoes, put them across our shoulders, and walked back to the end of the potato patch and started our rows.

"Six more rows. We ought to finish by five," my father said, leaning on his hoe handle and looking at his watch.

While we worked, Jerry-B growled like low thunder at the snake. He would try to crawl from one potato balk to the other, but Jerry-B would grab and try to hold on. The snake used both its mouth and its tail to drive him back two potato balks.

"That dog's got grit," my father bragged as we finished our rows and started back with two more. "He's the grittiest little dog I ever saw. But he's met his match."

"Look," I said as we hoed our rows out where the dog and snake were resting after another tussle. "The snake has gained six potato rows on Jerry-B."

"And look at our vines," he said.

The snake and dog had left a path of destruction across our potato patch where they had fought for every inch of ground. And the thunder was getting louder. A heavy cloud was hanging over Whetstone now.

"That's a rain cloud," my father said. "See how smooth and gray it is! Feel how much cooler the wind is. That wind is comin' from rain. We must hurry to finish before the rain!"

Before we had finished these rows, Jerry-B and the bull blacksnake tussled and rolled over more vines. They fought furiously to kill each other. We watch the potato vines fall as the snake and dog went end over end among them. When this fight stopped, Jerry-B lay flat on his belly on a clean balk and growled. He guarded the snake.

As we finished these two rows, the rain clouds were hanging over Sandy River. We could feel the rain in the wind. We could smell it. We knew it was coming. We worked hard and fast in the cooler wind as we started back in the last rows trying to beat the rain. Soon as we were back even with the dog and the snake, we counted the rows they had fought over. They had smashed the vines in a strip across the patch broad as a jolt-wagon road. They had fought over sixteen rows. Jerry-B was attacking furiously every time the snake tried to move.

In the distance, from our high hilltop, we could see the rain. It would soon be to the ridge top, but we would have our last rows hoed. Jerry-B was charging at the snake. We could see the snake striking back. He didn't strike with the same force he used at first. Both the snake and the dog were tiring. They were getting weak. We finished our rows and hurried across the potato patch to watch the finish. The lightning flashed around, the thunder roared over us like potato wagons across the skies.

The big snake was still trying to make it to the brush. He had only one more row to go. Jerry-B made a vicious attack. The snake used new tactics on the tired dog. He didn't offer to fight back now but crawled toward the brush with Jerry-B's saw-brier teeth fastened in its skin, holding with every ounce of strength he had. But the snake was so heavy he pulled the dog toward the brush.

"I'm goin' to kill that snake," I said, raising my hoe above my shoulder. "I'm not goin' to let him get away."

"No, you're not," my father said. "That snake deserves to live. He's a fighter. He's one of the few old residenters left. I don't like snakes, but I like him."

"If Jerry-B ever runs into this snake again, the fight will be renewed," I said. "My dog is a fighter too!"

As the snake reached the brush, with Jerry-B pulling back with all the strength in his tired body, it was not crawling much faster than a snail. Heavy torrents of rain began to fall. We started toward the tobacco barn as hard as we could go, for we were hot, and we didn't want to get too wet. Jerry-B gave his last pull in the rain, but the snake slipped from his mouth into the vast undergrowth that was its home.

This was the first time I had ever seen my father smile when a snake got away. This was the first time I'd ever seen him let a snake get away. It was the first time I'd ever seen him let anything trample his potato vines. But I didn't smile when I looked at Jerry-B walking beside us with his tongue almost touching the ground and his tail tucked between his legs. This was the first battle with a snake he had ever lost.

IV

Grandpa Birdwell's Last Battle

"Adger, now you hurry along and get up the Hollow to your Grandpa's," Ma said. "I hate to see your Grandma and Grandpa left alone in that old house after night. It might ketch fire and burn 'em up. Somebody might think they've got money and try to rob 'em. You hurry along and get there before dark."

"Mom, I'm gettin tired of goin up there every night," I said. "I get lonesome sittin before the fire and hearin Grandpa tell his big windy tales about fightin. Grandma will sit there beside him and listen to him tell the same tales over night after night. When Grandpa gets through tellin one of his big tales Grandma will say, "That's the truth. Battle's tellin you the truth."

"Your Grandpa has been a fightin man. I don't see any harm in him tellin about it. If you live long enough, you'll be doin the same thing. But you'll never be the man that your Grandpa has been. The country doesn't need the kind of men now that it needed then. The tough country made your Grandpa a tough man."

Grandpa never wore any shoes. When he got to tellin about one of his fights, and how he had the man by the throat with his big hand, his toes started wigglin. Then a frown came over Grandpa's face. He squirmed in his chair. And he took another drink from the jug. I didn't tell Ma about this. I didn't tell her how Grandma sipped moonshine with him from the jug. They called it "Honerable Herbs." Ma didn't know about it. I wouldn't tell anythin on Grandma and Grandpa if I didn't like what they were doin.

"Hurry along, Adger," Ma said. "The sun is goin down and shadows are lengthenin over the path. You might step on a snake."

I put my cap on my head and rolled my overalls to my knees. I started up the Hollow to Grandpa's house.

As I went up the Hollow, I walked under the shadows of the water-birches. I thought that sticks across my path were snakes. I thought the big gnarled roots that hove above the ground around the trunks of the big oaks and slippery-elms were piles of snakes.

"You're late, Adger," Grandpa said. "What's kept you so?"

"Was late gettin my work done," I said.

"We've missed you," Grandma said.

When Grandma said this, I was sorry about the way I'd talked about Grandpa and Grandma. I looked at Grandma's white hair and her wrinkled face. Her dim blue eyes looked across the table at Grandpa. He was sittin on the other side of the table with his legs crossed. He had his hand on the jug. His hair was white as cotton. Grandpa was sittin back in his chair like the world belonged to him. I could tell that he was gettin ready to brag about his fightin.

The white whiskey jug with the brown neck was on the table between them. There was a cup on the table for Grandma. Grandpa wouldn't sip his "Honerable Herbs" from a cup. He had to drink from the jug.

"Glad to see you, Adger, my son," Grandpa said. He looked at me with his sky-blue eyes. The white beard covered the wrinkles on Grandpa's face. I don't know whether his face was wrinkled or not. I don't believe it was. I never saw his face shaved.

"Guess you get kind of lonesome comin up here and stayin with us," Grandma said. "All the other boys air out fox huntin, giggin fish at the Sandy Falls and sparkin at the big revival meetins and kickin up their heels at the square dances."

"No, Grandma, I don't get lonesome," I said.

"I'll tell you where we miss it, Lizzie," Grandpa went on to say. "We ought to take Adger into our company and let him drink with us. That's why it's lonesome for Adger here."

"He's too young, Battle," Grandma said. "His Ma would take the roof off the house if she thought we'd give him a dram."

"Guess you air right, Lizzie," Grandpa said, as he reached for the jug.

Grandpa held the jug high in the air. He looked toward the newspapered ceiling as he drank. His Adam's apple worked up and down on his big beardy neck. Grandpa's big bare feet were turned toward me. The skin on the bottom of his feet was thick and tough where he had gone barefooted.

"I'll tell you that's good 'Herbs,' Lizzie," Grandpa said. " 'Herbs' like these wouldn't hurt Adger 'r any other young man. He's got a great experience comin. That will be when he partakes of the 'Herbs' and the world becomes his own."

"Yes, Battle," Grandma said as she poured a cup of 'Herbs' from the jug.

"That doesn't look like it's got much power to me," I said. "That looks like clear water, Grandma."

"Adger, sonny, it's everythin in the world but clear water," Grandma answered. "Two cups of this would make me want to stand on my head."

Grandma held her cup to her lips and sipped. She sipped like a cat drinks milk from a saucer. Grandpa watched Grandma sip her 'Herbs.' His mouth opened in a big smile. Grandpa laughed at Grandma the way she sipped her "Honerable Herbs."

"Here's the way to take it, Lizzie," Grandpa said as he lifted the jug to his lips. His Adam's apple worked up and down on his big bull-neck. After each swallow, he made a gurglin noise.

"Aham, aham," Grandpa said as he pulled the jug neck from his mouth. "I'll tell you, that's wonderful."

Grandpa placed the jug back on the table between him and Grandma.

"I wish he was older, Lizzie," Grandpa said. "I hate to have anybody around me too young to jine me when I have a drink of 'Herbs.' I like to have my company to jine me with a drink of 'Herbs' or a smoke of the fragrant weed."

"That reminds me, Battle," Grandma said as she pulled her long-stemmed clay pipe from her apron pocket. She tamped the terbacker crumbs in her pipe with her index finger. She held a stick of pine kindlin over the lamp globe until the resin began to ooze and it caught fire.

Grandma lit her pipe. She puffed a big cloud of smoke from her long-stemmed pipe.

[34]

"Wait a minute, Lizzie," Grandpa said. "Don't fan that stick of kindlin wood yet. Let it burn. I need it."

Grandpa reached in his inside coat pocket and pulled out a long green taste-bud terbacker cigar. Grandma bent over the table and laughed until she got strangled on smoke from her pipe.

"What's the matter with you, Lizzie?" Grandpa said. "Have you sipped too much of the 'Honerable Herbs'?"

"I'll tell you what I was thinkin about, Battle, if you won't get mad."

"Cross my heart and swear," Grandpa promised.

"I was just thinkin about the good times we're havin since all our children left us," Gandma said. "We thought we's goin to get lonesome without 'em. We've never been lonesome. We've been having the very best time of our lives ever since our dozen youngins left this nest."

"Now, Lizzie, that's not all you's laughin about," Grandpa said. "I know you too well. I know the things that touch your tickle bone."

"I just thought," Grandma said, "when you's lightin that cigar, what if you'd get your beard on fire and it would burn the beard off'n your face clean as a fire burns new ground. Wonder if your face would be burned black as new ground."

"That's what tickled you," Grandpa said. "I don't see anything funny enough to laugh about that. If my face was to get on fire it would be awful."

"You've done so much fightin in your day," Grandma laughed, "could you fight the fire on your face?"

"You've sipped too many 'Herbs,' " Grandpa said. "I'm sittin here thinkin about my fight with Bill Sexton."

[35]

I looked at Grandpa's toes. When he spoke of Bill Sexton, he wiggled his toes.

"Don't tell me about that fight you lost," Grandma pleaded to him. "Tell about fights you've winned."

"It's not fair to always be a winner, Lizzie," Grandpa said as he lifted the jug to his mouth again.

Gurgle, gurgle, gurgle, gurgle. Grandpa's Adam's apple worked up and down on his throat as he swallowed.

"Nothin in this world like it, Lizzie," Grandpa said as he put the jug back on the table and wiped the beard around his mouth with the back of his big hand. "It's powerful stuff, Lizzie. Watch your sippin."

"Tell us about Bill Sexton," I said. "What did he do to you, Grandpa?"

"What did he do to me?" Grandpa repeated.

Grandpa began to wiggle his toes. He jumped up from his chair and stood in the middle of the floor. He looked like a giant. His big arms swung down at his side. His big gnarled hands looked like shovels. His blue eyes beamed in the yellow lamplight. He looked straight ahead of him at the wall. His big feet flattened on the floor like a blowin viper's head when it hisses.

"Show Adger the scars on my head, Lizzie," Grandpa commanded.

Grandma stood up. She couldn't tip-toe and reach Grandpa's head to find the scars. She climbed up in her chair where she could part the white hair, thick and clean as a sheep's wool. She parted the hair until she found the big scar.

"Look where Bill Sexton hit your Grandpa with a coal pick that time," Grandma said. "Look what a scar he will carry to his grave."

"And to think I let him skip the country," Grandpa stormed. "I let him get away. I didn't follow him. I get so mad now that I could bite a ten-penny nail in two when I think of that man. I'd a got 'im but he knocked me out. I didn't wake up for two days."

Grandma climbed down out'n the chair and Grandpa sat down in his chair.

"I'll tell you," Grandpa said, "I've been a fightin man. I could stand a good fight right now. I ain't afraid of hell and high waters."

"Don't let Bill Sexton rile you," Grandma said. "He may be dead, you don't know. You run 'im out'n this country and we've never heard tell of 'im."

"Let 'im die," Grandpa shouted and wiggled his toes. "Let Bill Sexton die. He fouled me in a coal mine and you know it."

"You didn't have any business goin in that coal mine for Bill Sexton," Grandma answered. "You went in that coal bank to whop him and didn't have anything to fight with but your fist. He had a coal pick to fight you with and he used it. Hit you three times in the head with it. He could see you comin, for the light was behind you. You couldn't see him, for he was against the coal-vein."

"Yep, that's the way he got me," Grandpa said. "If I'd a-knowed he's goin to use a coal pick, I'd a-caved his damned ribs in is what I'd a-done."

"You've had too much 'Herbs,' Battle," Grandma said. "You air gettin riled."

"I'm not gettin riled," Grandpa said. "I'm already riled. I hope and pray to the Almighty that he comes back here one of these days. I'll whop him shore as the Saviour made little green pawpaws."

"It's been fifty-three years since you fit him, Battle," Grandma said.

Grandpa sat and wiggled his toes. He looked mean out'n his eyes.

"Think I'll get me a drink of water," Grandpa said.

"I'll get the water for you, Grandpa," I said.

"I'll get my own drinkin water, thank you," Grandpa said. "I'll be able to wait on myself yet."

"Battle's riled," Grandma said softly to me. "I tried to get him to talk about the men he had whopped instead of the men that whopped him."

Grandpa got up from his chair and started toward the kitchen. He had to cross the entry. The entry was once a dog-trot through Grandpa's house. They took the floor up and left a dirt floor. They used this entry in winter for a place to stack wood. The kitchen was on the other side of the entry.

I looked when Grandpa stepped down from the door into the entry. He was carryin a burning stick of kindlin wood for a light. The last thing I saw above his head was the lighted torch. The next thing I heard was Grandpa holler.

"Dad-durn you to hell nohow," he shouted. "I'll kill ye. Damn you to hell nohow, I'll kill ye!"

"Battle's in another fight," Grandma shouted. "It may be Bill Sexton."

Grandma grabbed the lamp in such a hurry that the globe fell off and smashed on the floor. I followed Grandma toward the entry.

"Fetch the light, Lizzie," Grandpa hollered. "Come here, Lizzie."

"Oh, my Lord, it's a snake," Grandma hollered as she

saw the dark entry and Grandpa fightin a snake. He was stompin it with one foot and it was holding his other foot with its fangs.

"He's got his teeth hung in my britches' leg," Grandpa shouted. "Damn ye to hell, you low-down sneak. You air as unfair as Bill Sexton. Crawl from under a man's floor and try to bite him."

"Kill him, Battle," Grandma shouted as she put the lamp on the floor and started clappin her hands. "Kill him, Battle! Tear him to pieces."

"He needs more light," I said as I picked the lamp up and held it so Grandpa could see.

"You air right, Adger," Grandpa said as he bent over and reached for the snake.

Before Grandpa could bend over and reach the big copperhead with his hand, it had let loose of his foot.

"Watch 'im, Battle," Grandma shouted. "He wants to bite your hand, Battle!"

"I'll get 'im, Lizzie," Grandpa said. "Don't you worry. I'll kill this low-down copperhead."

The snake writhed on the ground floor. Grandpa raised up and jumped two feet into the air to come down on the snake with both his bare feet. When he came back to the ground, the snake was coiled like a well-rope around a windlass. Grandpa missed the snake.

"Watch 'im, Battle," Grandma shouted. "Don't step on him and get snake bones in your feet. You won't live twenty-four hours if you do."

"I'll win this battle," Grandpa shouted to Grandma and looked up at her.

Whip!

[39]

The copperhead struck Grandpa on the other leg and let loose to get ready and strike again.

"Oh, my Lord, Battle," Grandma pleaded. "Leave that snake alone. It's riled and it ain't a-goin to quit fightin. It's atter you, Battle. It will finish you."

"I ain' begun to fight," Grandpa said. "I'm not whopped. I'll never let a little thing as a copperhead crawl into my house and start a fight with me. I feel like fightin tonight. This snake is the spirit of Bill Sexton—the only man I didn't whop."

"Whew—" Grandpa stomped at the copperhead and missed. It struck again at Grandpa and missed.

"Come on, Battle," Grandma clapped her hands and started over to help Grandpa.

"You can't do that," I said. I held her wrist with one hand and with the other I held the lamp.

"Bite me, you low-down scamp," Grandpa shouted. "I'm as full of pizen as you air."

Before the snake had time to make up his mind, Grandpa took a run and jumped at the snake. His big heel caught the copperhead on the flat head and squashed it. The snake writhed on the dusty floor with its head mashed into the dirt and its big bright body still alive, but not for long.

"I told you I'd whop this snake," Grandpa said proudly. "Bill Sexton is dead and his spirit had to go into somethin and it couldn't go into anythin higher than a snake."

"I'm so proud of you, Battle," Grandma said. "But I'm glad you did stomp that snake. I wonder if you've got them pizen copperhead ribs in your feet?"

"I'm bit all over nohow," Grandpa said as he climbed up the steps into the front room and Grandma took him by the arm.

"Do you want me to get you a drink of water, Grandpa?" I asked.

"Nope, I'll drink from my jug."

"That's right, Battle," Grandma said. "You need plenty of pizen in you."

Grandpa got the jug. I put the lamp back on the table.

"Gurgle, gurgle, gurgle, gurgle, gurgle."

"Drean the jug, Battle," Grandma said. "You've got a lot of pizen in you."

"Gurgle, gurgle, gurgle, gurgle, gurgle."

Grandpa put the jug on the table long enough to get his breath.

"Hurry, Battle, and get the 'Herbs' down you," Grandma warned.

"Give me time, Lizzie."

"I need to put the turpentine bottle to the places the copperhead bit you," Grandma said. "You'll wake up in the mornin and you'll never know you battled with a copperhead."

"Gurgle, gurgle, gurgle, gurgle, gurgle."

"I'm seein darkness, Lizzie," Grandpa said. "Lower me to the floor. Don't let me fall."

While I steadied Grandpa, Grandma put a quilt down on the floor and she put a pillow on the quilt. We lowered Grandpa to the quilt. He didn't speak after we got him down. He was lifeless as a tree.

"I'll get the turpentine," Grandma said.

By the time Grandma got back with the turpentine, I had found the two places where the copperhead had socked him.

"I'll get the light down there," Grandma said. "I want to see where the snake's teeth went in Battle's legs. It'll look like briar prints."

[41]

"Here's one place, Grandma. See, right here by Grandpa's ankle!"

"I can see the prints of its fangs."

Grandma put the unstopped bottle-neck down over the bite.

"Put the lamp up close, Adger," she said. "See if you can see any green stripes of pizen goin up into the turpentine bottle."

I got down on my all-fours. I stuck my face up against the bottle. I held the lamp close so I could see.

"I can see it, Grandma," I said. "I can see green stripes goin up in the turpentine bottle."

"I'll haf to hurry so I can draw the pizen from Battle's other leg."

"Here's the other bite, Grandma," I said. I showed her the place on Grandpa's shin bone.

Grandma carefully put the turpentine bottle over the place.

"Watch for the pizen, Adger,"

"I see plenty of it."

"I'll take the bottle away now," Grandma whispered. "It's almost full of copperhead pizen. Think I got about all the pizen. All I didn't get the 'Herbs' will get. Now you fetch me a quilt and I'll spread it over Battle and let him rest the night here."

I got a quilt off'n one of the beds for Grandma. She spread it over Grandpa.

"Battle's a brave old warrior," she said as she spread the quilt over him. "He'll fight anything that walks, crawls, or flies."

"Look, Grandma, his toes are wigglin under the kiver."

"He's fightin in his dreams."

"Reckon he's all right?"

"Of course he's all right," she said. "He's been bit before by copperheads. We know how to fight 'em."

We sat there and watched Grandpa's chest heave up and down as he got his breath and let it go again.

"Do you reckon that was Bill Sexton's spirit in that snake?" Grandma asked. "He was a sneak and the snake sneaked from under the floor and bit Battle near the ankle. That's the way Bill Sexton fit."

"I don't know whether it was Bill Sexton or not," I said. "I don't know whether a man can go into a snake when he dies."

"I believe he can," Grandma whispered. "That snake had the countenance of Bill Sexton."

We sat awhile by Grandpa's pallet.

"It's gettin late, Adger," Grandma said. "We'd better turn in and get a little sleep. I'll sleep here in the room where I can wait on Battle if he wants anything. You sleep upstairs where you've always slept."

"All right, Grandma."

I didn't sleep well. I dreamed of snakes runnin from a new-ground fire. I saw them go over the steep hill-slope with their heads high in the air and their tails barely touchin the ground. Grandpa was after them with a club. When Grandma called me down to breakfast, Grandpa was sittin at the table.

"We had some night last night, didn't we," he said.

"Yep, we did, Grandpa."

"I never had a better night's sleep than the one I had last night. I feel just like a two-year-old today."

"Battle, you winned a good fight last night."

Grandpa looked at Grandma and smiled.

"I believe it was Bill Sexton that I fit."

"It might have been Bill Sexton, Battle."

"If that snake was Bill Sexton," Grandpa said, "I'll be able to die happy when I die. I'm good for twenty more years yet."

Grandpa took a sup of coffee from his saucer.

V

Yoked for Life

&§|| "But you must not shudder and quiver when we talk about the livin' things of God's creation," Uncle Jeff said solemnly. "I know the subject of snakes is not a very polite one. And I know people don't want to hear about 'em. But why I brought up the subject of snakes is that it fits into a defect in our human society."

I didn't know what Uncle Jeff's line of thought for the evening conversation was going to be. But I knew when he got to talking about a favorite subject it was hard to get him stopped. He liked to talk, and when he started telling one of his favorite stories, he wouldn't stop . . . well, he might have stopped if we had got up and left the room.

"Now you take Old Seymour Pratt," Uncle Jeff said. "He's our neighbor and friend. How many wives do you think he's had?"

"Well, I can remember three," sister Mary said.

"I remember four of Seymour's wives," I said.

"I'm older than you, Shan," sister Sophia said. "I remember five."

"I remember Seymour's wife Bertha," Pa said. "I'm not nearly as old as Jeff. Bertha made six wives."

"He had one more," Uncle Jeff said. "Tillie Pruitt was his first wife."

"What happened to all of his wives?" brother Finn asked.

[45]

Now my brother Finn was nine years younger than I was. "I didn't know Seymour Pratt had so many wives," he went on. "What did he do with all of 'em?"

"Uncle Jeff, what has this got to do with snakes?" sister Glenna asked.

"It's got a lot to do with snakes," Uncle Jeff said.

"Stop interrupting your Uncle Jeff," Mom said. "Let him continue with his story. When brother Jeff talks, he always has something to say."

When Mom said this, Pa turned his head and smiled. Often when Uncle Jeff was talking at his best to us on the long winter evenings before the fire, he had had a little nip from his bottle. And Uncle Jeff's nipping was another story which he never told. But this was why he was living with us. He had been married and was the father of eight children. They were all married now and had homes of their own. And his wife, Aunt Mettie, was dead. Before her death, she and Uncle Jeff had lived apart for twenty years. They were never divorced, but they were separated. She stayed in their old home, and Uncle Jeff came to live with us.

"Now, you asked about old Seymour's wives," Uncle Jeff continued. "Three are dead; four are livin'. I guess old Seymour and his seventh wife, Hattie Sprouse Pratt, are havin' some awful battles. I hear they've been in court, but Judge Rivercomb shamed old Seymour and told him he'd had enough wife trouble and to settle down and behave himself. Now old Seymour's troubles have caused me to think of snakes. And right now I'm thinkin' of the copperhead."

"Oh, Jeff," Mom said, "Why bring up the copperhead?"

"Because the copperhead is the meanest snake, the most dangerous and deadly of all snakes we have in these here parts," Uncle Jeff said. "Remember, Mollie, when a copperhead bit you? You disturbed him, didn't you? You reached your hand under a tobacco stalk to pull the grass away, and you put your hand right on him. He was under the cool leaves away from the summer sun takin' his afternoon nap. You scared him, and he bit your hand. Once I was plowin' tobacco and stepped on one beside a rock in the tobacco balk. He jumped up from his sleep and grabbed my leg. But we lived, Mollie! And I like to think we lived for a purpose. See, we look at any kind of snake as bein' somethin' evil, don't we? And we think there is more evil in the copperhead, because he's the meanest of all snakes."

"I agree with you, Jeff," my father said.

My father seldom agreed with Uncle Jeff on anything. And maybe the reason was that he could never tell a story like Uncle Jeff. But we liked to hear Uncle Jeff talk.

Uncle Jeff was a big man. He weighed 307 pounds. He was six feet two and there were no bulges on his powerful body. He was a muscular man, with arms as big as small fence posts, legs at the calves as big as gate posts, and hands as big as shovels. His big head sat almost squarely on his shoulders, and a stranger had to look twice to see if he had any neck. He had a kind face and big blue eyes. His head was bald on top and there was a rim of white hair around the base of his head. He had to have shirts, shoes, gloves, and pants made-to-order. The only ready-made clothes he could buy to fit him were a necktie and a hat. We had to make a special chair for him to sit on, and once one of our beds broke down while he was in it asleep.

A person who had never seen Uncle Jeff before might have thought he was as mean among men as the copperhead was among snakes. But Uncle Jeff didn't hunt and he wouldn't kill anything. He wouldn't even kill a poisonous copperhead. Once in the field I saw him shoo one away.

"Why did you do that, Uncle Jeff?" I asked.

"It was put here for a purpose," he told me quickly. "Besides, the copperhead has his own enemies."

"Who are his enemies?"

"The blacksnake and the terrapin. And man isn't exactly friendly to the copperhead either."

Now Uncle Jeff resumed his story, "The copperheads wed for life," he said, looking up at the ceiling. "Oh, I'm not sure whether a pair might separate or not. I suppose they do. But when the he-copperhead gets killed, the she-copperhead becomes a widow. And if the she-copperhead gets squeezed to death by a blacksnake, or chewed to death by a stud-terrapin, then the he-copperhead becomes a widower. The love life is all over for them. See, our Creator put them here to point the way of deep and abidin' love."

"Now, Jeff, you're going too far," Pa said.

"Mick, let Jeff tell his story," Mom said. "He has more to tell. If you give Jeff time, he will prove his point."

"Yes, I have more to tell, and I will prove my point," Uncle Jeff continued. "And . . ."

"But I don't believe copperheads love like that," Pa interrupted.

"Just listen until I finish, Mick," Uncle Jeff said.

"Yes, let Uncle Jeff go on," I said.

"We do want to know about snake-love," Sophia said. My oldest sister, Sophia, was old enough to be having dates now. She could hardly keep from laughing at Uncle Jeff.

"Now, back in Elliott County, a young couple got married," Uncle Jeff said. "You remember John Porter and Ann Cox?"

"Yes, Jeff, I do," Mom interrupted. "I know what you're going to tell now. Go ahead and tell us."

"Well, John Porter was our fourth cousin and Ann Cox was some distant cousin to us—eighth, ninth, or maybe a tenth cousin," Uncle Jeff said. "Before they married back in them days, it was customary to have the house built enough so they could move in. So the parents of the young couple cut trees to make logs for the walls. They sawed clapboards from tall straight oaks to make a roof. They split chestnut puncheons for the floor. And they built the house in about a week. After the bellin', John and Ann went straight to their new house. One of their parents had given them a featherbed, pillows, and quilts—and the other's parents had given them a stove! You know how it used to be, Mollie. The parents of the bride and groom gave them the basic necessities to start housekeepin' on. Their parents gave them a cow for milk and hens to lay eggs. See, in them days people had to dig a livin' from the ground, or starve, and it wasn't easy to live farmin' the steep Elliott County hills.

"Well, John and Ann Porter were a nice-lookin' couple," Uncle Jeff said. "John was a tall, powerful man and handy with an ax, and Ann was a medium-sized buxom woman with bright blue eyes. I'll never forget her eyes so long as I live. I was a saplin' of a boy then, and I thought she was the prettiest young woman in Elliott County. They were married in April, and they moved into their new house just after the weddin' and after we belled them there that night. I remember the house wasn't finished, but it didn't matter, for they were in a hurry to move into their new home. Back in them days, people weren't afraid of a few cracks between the logs, especially in April when the wind was warm and fresh. And, of course, they had planned to have the cracks chinked and have mud daubed over the chinkin' before the cold autumn nights.

"Well, John cleared the ground and planted a crop of corn, tobacco, and wheat the first spring," Uncle Jeff continued with his story while we listened eagerly. He spoke words we could catch and hold just like somebody putting rocks into a bucket. They were there, and they were solid. Uncle Jeff could tell it better than anyone could write it down.

"April, May, and June passed. There was consistent love between them, John and Ann. And I remember seein' them ride all hugged up in a little hug-me-tight buggy to the store in Bruin. They traded eggs for groceries, and they had some money to spend. Their corn grew tall and their wheat grew up and ripened until a high slope looked from far off like a sheet of gold. Their tobacco grew tall, and the leaves were broad and dark. John was a good farmer. And Ann helped him some in the fields. She helped him until their first child was on the way.

"Now August come, and if you don't know it, I do know that August is a bad month for snakes. The hot sun beamed down in Elliott County in August, and just about everybody hunted shade. The minnows in the mountain streams found a shady pool of water; the groundhogs went back into their dirt holes where it was cool. They stirred early in the mornin' before the sun was up, or in the late afternoon when the sun went down. And the squirrels stirred early and late too, and slept in their nests in the shade or deep in holes in the hollow trees when the sun was up. The snakes found cool places to coil and sleep, and they stirred about mostly at night when it was cool. They foraged for food at night in the dense dark woods and overgrown fields.

"One August night when the weather was very hot and the wind didn't come through the cracks and windows in John and Ann's house, John thought he heard a noise like a broom swishin' over the puncheon floor.

" 'Ann, do you hear somethin'?' John whispered.

" 'Yes, I'm awake, listenin' to it, John,' she whispered. 'Couldn't be somebody here, could it?'

" 'I'll see,' he whispered.

"Since John kept a kerosene lamp on a chair beside his bed, and a box of matches by the lamp, he struck a match and lit the lamp. 'Ann, Ann!' he said, 'don't look!' But Ann did look at the big copperhead crawlin' slowly over the puncheon floor toward the bed.

" 'I told you not to look, Ann,' he said. You see," Uncle Jeff explained, "when a pregnant woman looks at a snake, the snake will go blind.

"The snake stopped suddenly after Ann looked at him, held his head in the air, and moved it around and around like he was addled. Then John got out of bed and shined the lamplight in the snake's eyes, and sure enough he was blind. His once beady black eyes in their lidless sockets were like clots of phlegm.

" 'Sorry, darlin',' John said to his wife, 'but you blinded him.'

" 'But you plan to kill him anyway, John,' she said.

" 'No, I planned to shoo him out with the broom,' John

[51]

told her. 'I'm afraid to kill a snake. I let them snakes kill each other.'

" 'John, that's crazy talk,' she told him. 'You're a big strong he-man! You got too much sense to think like that.'

" 'Haven't you heard, darlin', that the copperhead is filled with the damned souls of evil men? There is more evil in that snake than you might think. Since you have blinded him, I'm goin' to shoot that snake. Stop your ears with your finger, darlin'.'

"John lifted the squirrel rifle down from the joints where he kept it hangin' above the bed. He took aim at the copperhead's neck when it stopped movin'. Then he fired and the snake went limp on the floor. The bullet almost severed its neck, and passed on through the green chestnut puncheon floor and went into the ground, under the house.

" 'I never saw a snake bleed like that one,' John told Ann. And if you don't know this, when a snake bleeds a lot, it's not exactly the snake's blood that pours forth," Uncle Jeff said. "That blood is supposed to be the blood of all the damned that has become a part of the snake. John Porter knew this.

"So that night John took the snake over to Clem Worthington's shack," Uncle Jeff continued. "Clem was an old man, whose wife was dead, and he now lived alone. Many people thought he was a Wise One. He read the stars, coffee cups, and studied nature, and he read Hosea, the prophet, until he had begun to think he was a prophet. He told the people he was a prophet and they believed him. And to tell you the truth," Uncle Jeff said, with a sigh, "it was Old Clem that first put me onto the constancy of snake love. It was Old Clem who said the snake was more sacred

than people thought and that the Creator put him here
for a purpose, or he wouldn't be on this earth. Well, what
he had said made sense to me.

"I can see Old Clem yet in his little two-room house
with weeds growin' high as the porch was tall. He sat in a
little room with his books all around him, and he took long
walks the four seasons of the year. He observed the Creator's
handiwork and he tried to figure things out to his own
satisfaction and for his people. He called us his people, and
I guess we were. Old Clem has long gone to his reward. He
sleeps on an Elliott County hill without a marker on his
grave. Well, I went back there, and I couldn't find it. And
this reminds me of a truth he once said—that man wasn't
as immortal as a grain of sand. He said a grain of sand went
on forever, but man disappeared from the earth. And poor
Old Clem, by dyin', has proved his point.

"But the night John shot the copperhead, he took the
varmint to Old Clem and told him how Ann, who was with
child, looked at the snake and how its eyes turned to clots
of phlegm as she looked, and how he shot it instead of
shooin' it out with a broom as he had planned. He told
Old Clem that he was scared after the way it bled.

" 'You had better be scared,' Old Clem told him. 'You
and Ann are in for serious trouble. I could mention a half
dozen evil men, cutthroats, murderers, and robbers, who
might be hidin' in this here snake.'

"John Porter, who was young, big and powerful, and un-
afraid of man or animal, now stood before Old Clem
shakin' like an oak leaf in the night wind.

" 'Rufus Johnson, who knocked old Jerry Bruck in the
head for his money, is in that snake,' Old Clem told John.

'Old Mary Howes, who tolled Flem Berry to the rock-cliff where Tom and Boz Bean were waitin' to murder him, is in that there snake. Old Fose Jones, so mean to an animal he'd beat his mule's eye out with a stick—I'm sure he is there, too. Thurmond Turnipseed, who killed four men for the love of killin', is surely in him. Erf Springhill, who shot his own father, is there. It is their blood, John, that spilled when you shot the snake,' Old Clem told John. 'You've unleashed all this evil upon us. The copperhead holds the evil, and should be left for other snakes to kill.'

" 'I told Ann that,' said John. 'She didn't believe.'

" 'She will believe,' Old Clem told him. 'She might be killed and you might be killed with her, since you are yoked together by the Creator's Divine Law.'

" 'What will I do with this dead snake?' John asked.

" 'It don't matter now,' said Clem. 'As you ride back, throw him off in the weeds. All the evil he held has gone into his mate. She'll take up the fight.'

" 'You may be the wisest of all men around here,' John said, 'but I can hardly believe all this. How can evil go from evil back to evil?'

" 'You will see,' Old Clem warned him. 'Throw the dead snake away. It isn't as much as a grain of sand now. It won't go back to a little grain of sand, but it will go back to loam and nothin' will grow from that there loam for three years. It will kill everythin' close to it. Take that evil carcass out of here, John.'

"John took the snake and threw it in a weedpatch beside the path as he rode his mule back home."

"Jeff, you're making all this up," Pa said. "It's the wildest story I ever heard. No man in his right senses will believe that stuff."

[54]

"No, Brother Jeff isn't making it up," Mom said. "I know the story. Everybody up in Elliott County knew it."

"All right, if I am makin' up a bunch of lies, I'll stop my story, Mick," Uncle Jeff said. "I don't like to speak before an unbeliever."

"Go on with the story, Uncle Jeff," I said. "I believe you because I want to believe you. I want to hear all the story."

"Yes, Uncle Jeff, tell the rest of it," Sophia said.

But Uncle Jeff sat there for a minute. Brother Finn begged him to tell the rest. Mary begged him to go on, and then Glenna, our baby sister, wanted to hear all of the story. We liked to hear Uncle Jeff tell stories. We'd seen copperheads, and I had killed them. But now I wondered whether I would ever cut one's head off with a hoe again and unleash all that powerful evil. I had killed them because I was afraid of a copperhead. But now I thought of all the evil I might have unleashed, as I thought back about how each time I had killed a copperhead something dreadful had happened in our neighborhood. About the time I'd killed one, a man was stabbed to death. And at another time, a neighbor's barn burned with all his livestock in it. I thought the evil men were sealed up in a copperhead, like poison was sealed in a bottle.

"Now what started all of this was Old Seymour Pratt and his seven wives," Uncle Jeff said. "I say that the copperhead snake was put on this earth for a purpose. And that purpose for mankind might be to teach constant love. See, there is the frivolous love like Old Seymour has, or he wouldn't have had seven wives. When the copperhead takes his bride, it is a lifetime proposition with him! Now, Mick, if you won't interrupt me again, I'll continue . . ."

[55]

"All right, Jeff, you win," Pa said. "The children want to hear that crazy stuff, and I don't think it will contaminate their minds to listen to you. But my mind is closed to it."

"Contaminate their minds?" Uncle Jeff repeated in a surprised tone of voice. "It should help them. All of your children, Mick, my little nieces and nephews gathered around their old uncle listenin' to his voice now, will be proud some day that they had the opportunity to listen. They will be choosin' mates some day. Let's hope your sons won't be Seymour Pratts and that they and your daughters will choose mates for all eternity."

Pa shook his head disgustedly and leaned back in his chair.

"The news of Ann's blindin' that there snake and John's shootin' it and it bleedin' and him goin' to wise Old Clem in the night with the dead snake was narrated all over that there community the next day," Uncle Jeff said. "John told the story to Bill Wilcox, and when Bill went to Bruin to Jeff Harper's store, Bill told the story to Old Jeff, which was like puttin' it in the *Elliott County News*. That very night when John and Ann went to bed, John lit the lamp.

" 'John, I can't sleep with the light on,' Ann said. 'I like to lie in the dark and feel the night wind come through the cracks, and then I can sleep.'

" 'Darlin', something else might come through the cracks,' John said.

" 'What are you talkin' about?' she asked.

" 'The mate to that there snake I shot last night,' he replied.

" 'John, who told you that?' Ann asked. 'That old bag of wind you call wise Old Clem?'

" 'Yes, Old Clem told me,' he said. 'When I left here last night with the dead snake, you were asleep. Old Clem told me the mate might take revenge. And now, since the snake bled like it did, it was carryin' the souls of the damned and the evil—no fewer than seven, accordin' to what Old Clem said. He even named them last night.'

" 'John, are you losin' your mind?'

" 'I hope not.'

" 'Well, I can't sleep with that light on,' she said. 'Besides, we have to be rested to do the work ahead of us tomorrow.'

" 'If we don't keep the lamp burnin', that there copperhead's mate might come back to undo us. She will take her revenge, for I killed her mate, and copperheads wed for life.'

" 'I'm goin' to blow the lamp out so I can sleep,' Ann told John. 'I'm not afraid, because all that crazy talk goes in at one ear and comes out at the other.'

" 'You're takin' a chance,' John told her. 'And since you and I are yoked by the Creator's Divine Law, I'm in danger with you.'

"Ann blew out the lamp and she went to sleep in the dark while John lay on the bed and tossed. So he told me the next day when I went over there to borrow a hoe.

"What I wanted to find out was about his killin' the snake. He told me the story and he said he felt too tired to go to work in the tobacco, pullin' suckers from the stalks. He said he'd not had enough sleep. And he told me how Ann had got up that mornin', laughin'. Then at the breakfast table she had said to him, 'Well, the mate, the constant lover, didn't get up last night, did she?'

"And John told me his wife accused him of bein' teched

in the head. But I told Ann the mate could still come back on the second or the third night. And she laughed more than at any time since they'd been married. She even said her lookin' at the copperhead hadn't blinded him, but that this was a season called 'dog days' and all snakes went blind in dog days and regained their sight after the season was over.

"Well, this was the last time, Mick, I ever talked to John Porter, my fourth cousin," Uncle Jeff said. "Next time I saw John Porter, he was lyin' beside Ann, and they were dressed in their weddin' clothes, side by side in a big double coffin that Pap and the other men made for them. Not just the two of them but there was a third one, too. Their unborn went with its mother, Ann. It was on the third night that the old she-copperhead had followed her mate. She crawled through the crack of the cabin and found her mate's bloodstain on the puncheon floor. Then she sought revenge. She crawled up in the bed with John and Ann, and she must have bit one and then the other. Birdie Crump went over to help John sucker his tobacco the next morning, since they were exchangin' work. Birdie knew John got up early. Well, he waited around outside from six until seven. He watched the flue from the cookstove for smoke. There was no fire in the stove. Ann was not gettin' breakfast. So Birdie knocked on the door and no one answered. In those days, every man kept his huntin' gun handy by his bed, but no one ever locked a door. It was a disgrace and showed a man's cowardice. So Birdie just eased the door open and went in. He saw John and Ann still in bed. He spoke to them, but there was no answer. And he walked back to the bed and looked at their pale silent faces.

They weren't breathin'. Just as he was about to touch John's forehead to see if he was really dead, the old she-copperhead poked her head right up between them from under the cover. Birdie said, 'I jumped three steps backward in one hop. I took off to notify the neighbors.' I remember when Birdie came and told Pap; he was short of breath from runnin' and he was a scared man," Jeff continued. Jeff shook his head sadly. I thought he was going to cry.

"When Coroner Waterfield went to the cabin, the old she-copperhead had gone. She had come to the cabin with all her evil intent, and she had done her duty. John had been bitten four times, and Ann had been bitten six. They had been bitten early in the night when they were asleep, and the dose of poison injected in them was so much they were dead before mornin'. Well, we had a big funeral! You remember the funeral, don't you, Mollie?"

"Yes, I was a little girl, nine or ten, but I went to that funeral," Mom said. "That was the first and only time I ever saw a man and his wife buried in the same coffin."

"Now, Mick, what do you think of that?" Uncle Jeff asked Pa. "Do you believe copperheads are yoked for life? Do you believe in the constancy of their love?"

"Jeff, it doesn't matter what I believe," Pa told him quickly. "I keep a good sharp hoe for the copperheads. I think a man's greatest problem in staying married to the woman he loves is her relatives. I wonder if the the copperhead snakes have relatives that are as big pests as we have among the relatives in our human family."

Pa got up from his chair and rubbed his sleepy eyes. "I believe I'll turn in after that one, Jeff," he said. "You've really told one tonight."

"Mick, you don't appreciate brother Jeff," Mom said.

"I'm sure glad it's wintertime and the copperheads have hibernated," I said. "If it was summertime, I'd light the lamp upstairs and keep it lit all night, too."

"Yes, they're put here for a purpose, just like Old Clem used to tell us," Uncle Jeff sighed as he got up from his special chair Pa had made for him, so he wouldn't break all Mom's chairs. "The Creator had in mind a purpose for every livin' thing. And I believe the copperhead was put here to point the way to constant and abidin' love."

"What about Seymour Pratt, Uncle Jeff?" I asked. "Since he's had seven wives, will he join the six evil men and one woman in that old she-copperhead?"

"Son, I can't judge," Uncle Jeff said.

"I'm never sure of many things," Pa said, "but I'm sure of one thing. If Old Seymour is confined with the six evil men and one woman in the belly of that old copperhead, evil or no evil, not one of the six men would have a chance, for Old Seymour will get Old Mary! You can bet on that! I know him. Come on, and let's everybody get in bed before Jeff spins another one."

VI

Love

◆§|| Yesterday, when the bright sun blazed down on the wilted corn, my father and I walked around the edge of the new ground to plan a fence. The cows kept coming through the chestnut oaks on the cliff and running over the young corn. They bit off the tips of the corn and trampled down the stubble.

My father walked in the cornbalk. Bob, our collie, walked in front of my father. We heard a ground squirrel whistle down over the bluff among the dead treetops at the clearing's edge. "Whoop, take him, Bob," said my father. He lifted up a young stalk of corn, with wilted dried roots, where the ground squirrel had dug it up for the sweet grain of corn left on its tender roots. This has been a dry spring and the corn has kept well in the earth where the grain has sprouted. The ground squirrels love this corn. They dig up rows of it and eat the sweet grains. The young corn stalks are killed and we have to replant the corn.

I can see my father keep sicking Bob after the ground squirrel. He jumped over the corn rows. He started to run toward the ground squirrel. I, too, started running toward the clearing's edge where Bob was jumping and barking. The dust flew in tiny swirls behind our feet. There was a cloud of dust behind us.

[61]

"It's a big bull blacksnake," said my father. "Kill him, Bob! Kill him, Bob!"

Bob was jumping and snapping at the snake so as to make it strike and throw itself off guard. Bob had killed twenty-eight copperheads this spring. He knows how to kill a snake. He doesn't rush to do it. He takes his time and does the job well.

"Let's don't kill the snake," I said. "A blacksnake is a harmless snake. It kills poison snakes. It kills the copperhead. It catches more mice from the fields than a cat."

I could see the snake didn't want to fight the dog. The snake wanted to get away. Bob wouldn't let it. I wondered why it was crawling toward a heap of black loamy earth at the bench of the hill. I wondered why it had come from the chestnut oak sprouts and the matted greenbriars on the cliff. I looked as the snake lifted its pretty head in response to one of Bob's jumps. "It's not a bull blacksnake," I said. "It's a she-snake. Look at the white on her throat."

"A snake is an enemy to me," my father snapped. "I hate a snake. Kill it, Bob. Go in there and get that snake and quit playing with it!"

Bob obeyed my father. I hated to see him take this snake by the throat. She was so beautifully poised in the sunlight. Bob grabbed the white patch on her throat. He cracked it against the wind only. The blood spurted from her fine-curved throat. Something hit against my legs like pellets. Bob threw the snake down. I looked to see what had struck my legs. It was snake eggs. Bob had slung them from her body. She was going to the sand heap to lay her eggs, where the sun is the setting-hen that warms them and hatches them.

Bob grabbed her body there on the earth where the red blood was running down on the gray-piled loam. Her body was still writhing in pain. She acted like a greenweed held over a new-ground fire. Bob slung her viciously many times. He cracked her limp body against the wind. She was now limber as a shoestring in the wind. Bob threw her riddled body back on the sand. She quivered like a leaf in the lazy wind, then her riddled body lay perfectly still. The blood colored the loamy earth around the snake.

"Look at the eggs, won't you?" said my father. We counted thirty-seven eggs. I picked an egg up and held it in my hand. Only a minute ago there was life in it. It was an immature seed. It would not hatch. Mother Sun could not incubate it on the warm earth. The egg I held in my hand was almost the size of a quail's egg. The shell on it was thin and tough and the egg appeared under the surface to be a watery egg.

"Well, Bob, I guess you see now why this snake couldn't fight," I said. "It is life. Stronger devour the weaker even among human beings. Dog kills snake. Snake kills birds. Birds kill the butterflies. Man conquers all. Man, too, kills for sport."

Bob was panting. He walked ahead of us back to the house. His tongue was out of his mouth. He was tired. He was hot under his shaggy coat of hair. His tongue nearly touched the dry dirt and white flecks of foam dripped from it. We walked toward the house. Neither my father nor I spoke. I still thought about the dead snake. The sun was going down over the chestnut ridge. A lark was singing. It was late for a lark to sing. The red evening clouds floated above the pine trees on our pasture hill. My father stood beside the path. His black hair was moved by the wind. His face was red in the blue wind of day. His eyes looked toward the sinking sun.

"And my father hates a snake," I thought.

I thought about the agony women know of giving birth. I thought about how they will fight to save their children. Then I thought of the snake. I thought it was silly for me to think such thoughts.

The next morning, my father and I got up with the chickens. He says one has to get up with the chickens to do a day's work. We got the posthole digger, ax, spud, measuring pole and the mattock. We started for the clearing's edge. Bob didn't go along.

The dew was on the corn. My father walked behind with the posthole digger across his shoulder. I walked in front. The wind was blowing. It was a good morning wind to breathe and a wind that makes one feel like he can get under the edge of a hill and heave the whole hill upside down.

I walked out the corn row where we had come yesterday afternoon. I looked in front of me. I saw something. I saw it move. It was moving like a huge black rope winds around a windless. "Steady," I says to my father. "Here is the bull blacksnake." He took one step up beside me and stood. His eyes grew wide apart.

"What do you know about this," he said.

"You have seen the bull blacksnake now," I said. "Take a good look at him! He's lying beside his dead mate. He has come to her. He, perhaps, was on her trail yesterday."

The male snake had trailed her to her doom. He had come in the night, under the roof of stars, as the moon shed rays of light on the quivering clouds of green. He had found his lover dead. He was coiled beside her, and she was dead.

The bull blacksnake lifted his head and followed us as we walked around the dead snake. He would have fought us to his death. He would have fought Bob to his death. "Take a stick," said my father, "and throw him over the hill so Bob won't find him. Did you ever see anything to beat that? I've heard they'd do that. But this is my first time to see it." I took a stick and threw him over the bank into the dewy sprouts on the cliff.

VII

Word and the Flesh

◄§‖ Groan leads the way along the cow path; his disciples follow. The cow path is narrow, the pawpaw bushes are clustered on both sides of the path and they are wet with dew. Brother Sluss pulls a pawpaw leaf and licks off the sweet dew with his tongue. Brother Sluss is like a honeybee. The moon floats in the sky like a yellow pumpkin, dark yellowish like the insides of a pumpkin.

Groan and his disciples—Brothers Sluss, Frazier, Shinliver, Littlejohn, Redfern and Pigg—are headed for the Kale Nelson Graveyard. It is approximately one mile away, across Phil Hogan's cow pasture, Ben Lowden's pig lot, Cy Penix's corn patch, thence through the Veil Abraham's peach orchard to a flat where the ribs of an old house (the old Abraham's house) are bleached by the autumn sun and cooled by the autumn night wind. The robe Groan wears is similar to the robe Sunday-school cards picture Christ wearin when He walked and talked with His disciples. It has a low neck, loose flowin sleeves. It is long and tied with a sash at the waist line. The loose sleeves catch on the pawpaw twigs along the path.

"Tell me more about the ten virgins, Brother Groan."

"I don't know about the ten virgins and I ain't discussin the ten virgins. You know there was ten of them, don't

[67]

you? And you know one of them was Virgin Mary, don't you?"

"Yes, I know that, Brother Groan. But tell me more about them."

"Brother Sluss, we have other things to talk about. Leave me be, won't you? I want to talk with God. I want to feel the sperit. I want to show you what Faith will do to-night. Leave me alone. I am talkin to God now. I am in God's presence. Leave me be, will you?" Brother Groan carries a bundle under one arm. He carries a walkin staff in one hand. His loose sleeves are hard to get between the pawpaw twigs alongside the path.

There is silence. Brother Groan talks to God. They keep movin. They come to the drawbars. One by one they slip between the drawbars, all but Brother Frazier. He is too thick to slip between the rails. He crawls under the bottom rail. Now they are goin through Ben Lowden's pig lot. The moon above them is pretty in the sky. It is still a yellow pumpkin moon—that darkish yellow, the color of the insides of a ripe sun-cooked cornfield pumpkin. The dew on the crab grass in the pig lot sparkles in the yellow moonlight. The September wind slightly rustles the half-way dead pawpaw bushes. The crickets sing, the katydids sing, the whippoorwills quirt-quirt and the owl who-whoos. Brother Groan mutters—an Unknown Tongue whispers to God.

"Brother Groan is goin to show us the Faith tonight."

"Brother Groan is talkin to God."

"No. That is the wind over there in Cy Penix's ripe corn. That is the wind in the corn blades talkin. That is not Sweet Jesus talkin."

"Be quiet, won't you? Brother Groan is tryin to talk to God."

"I ain't said nothin."

"No."

"It is the wind in the fodder blades, I tell you."

"The wind!"

"Didn't I say the wind?"

"Yes, you said the wind."

"Then why did you ask?"

"Because I thought that you said that Brother Sluss said that God whispered."

Brother Groan is first to mount the rail fence. His sleeve catches on one of the stakes-and-riders, but he gets over into Cy Penix's cornfield first. One by one his disciples climb over the fence. Here is the ripe uncut corn in the yellowish wine-colored moonlight. The dead blades are whisperin somethin. Maybe it is: "The dead lie buried here, the dead of ever-so-long-ago. But they lie buried here under the dead roots of this ripe corn."

The corn blades whisper to the wind. There is a sweet dew on these corn blades for Brother Sluss to lick off with his tongue. This dead fodder is buff-colored in the yellow-ish pumpkin-colored moonlight. Brother Groan leads his disciples through the field of dead corn. There is a ghostly chill of night piercin the thin robe of Brother Groan, and the overalls and the unbuttoned shirts of his disciples.

There is a loneliness in the night, in the moonlight that covers the land and in the wind among the trees. There is something lonely about dead leaves rakin against one's clothes at night, for they too seem to say: "The dead lie buried here, the dead of ever-so-long-ago. But they lie buried here under the livin roots of these autumn trees."

Lonely is the quirt-quirt of the whippoorwill, the song of the grasshopper and the katydid. And there is somethin lonely about dead fodder blades—the way they rake against the wind at night.

"Does God talk, Brother Littlejohn?"

"W'y yes, God talks. Ain't you got no Faith?"

"How do you know?"

"Because it is in the Word."

"Be quiet, please."

"It is the wind in the dead fodder."

"Are you sure that is all?"

"Yes."

"No."

"Why no?"

"It is Brother Groan feelin the sperit."

"How do you know?"

"I saw him jump up and down right out there before me."

"I saw him too jump up and down out there in the path. I saw his sleeve catch on the brush. I saw him in the moonlight."

"He is feelin the sperit then."

The peach orchard is not a new set of teeth. Too many of the teeth are gone if each tree is a tooth. Many of them are snaggled teeth too. Brother Groan walks under the peach trees too, and the good teeth and the bad teeth chew at his robe. Brother Groan gets along. The dead leaves hangin to the peach trees are purple. One cannot tell tonight. But come look tomorrow afternoon when the sun is shinin. There are half-dead leaves on the trees and whole-dead leaves on the trees. The wind fingers with the leaves. Brother Groan's sleeve has caught on the tooth of a peach tree. Brother Sluss hurries to free him. The sleeve is free now. The disciples move on. Brother Groan is silent.

"Where are we goin, Brother Shinliver?"

"To the Kale Nelson Graveyard."

"What for?"

"Brother Groan is goin to show us the Faith in the Word."

"How?"

"I don't know."

"By the Word?"

"No!"

"How?"

"I told you once I didn't know."

"Is that you talkin, Brother Redfern?"

"No."

"I thought I heard somebody."

"That was the wind you heard."

"Yes, that was the wind."

"Yes, that was the wind in the peach-tree leaves."

"Ain't we about there?"

"About where?"

"Kale Nelson Graveyard?"

"Right up there!"

"Right up where?"

"Right up there—see them white tombstones! That is the Kale Nelson Graveyard."

The moon is high above the Kale Nelson Graveyard and the wind is down close to the earth on this high flat. The dead weeds rattle. The dead grass is whisperin somethin.

Maybe it is: "The dead lie buried here. The dead of ever-so-long-ago. They lie buried here under our roots. We know the dead lie buried here." The loose leaves rustle in the wind. The moon is still big as a pumpkin floatin in the pretty night sky. The moon is still the color of the insides of a pumpkin.

Across the bones of the old house, Groan and his disciples go. The myrtle is vined around the old logs. There is a pile of stones here, a pile of stones over there. Here is the butt of an old field-stone chimney. There is a gate-post half-rotted. Ramble rose vines climb halfway up the rotted post. Here is a bushy-top yard tree with hitchin rings stapled in the sides. Here is a patch of blackberry briars. The wind blows through the blackberry briars and the blackberry briars scratch the wind. You ought to hear this wind whistle when it is scratched by the briars. If the wind dies, it cannot be buried here where the dead weeds whisper: "The dead lie under our roots, here in the Kale Nelson Graveyard." If Brother Groan dies, he can be buried here. Brother Groan is the kind of dead, when he does die, a grave can hold. Listen: Brother Groan is goin to speak now: "Gather around me, ye men of the Faith. Gather around me, ye men of God. Gather around me here. I want to show you there is power in the Word. Gather around me and let your voices speak in the Unknown Tongue to God."

Here on the myrtle-mantled logs of the old Abraham's house, men are groanin—men are cryin to God. They are pleadin to God. They are mutterin quarter words, half words and whole words to God. It is in the Unknown Tongue. Brother Sluss is on the ground now. He rolls out

[72]

into the graveyard. He breaks down the dead weeds that just awhile ago whispered to the wind that the dead lay under their roots. Brother Sluss smashes weeds half-dead like a barrel of salt rollin over them. Brother Sluss is a barrel-bellied man. He rolls like a barrel. Brother Little-john's pants have slipped below his buttocks. Brother Shin-liver is holdin to a tombstone and jerkin. Brother Frazier is pattin the ground with his shovel hands and cryin to God. Brother Groan is cryin to God. He faces the yellow moon and he cries to God. "Come around me, men, come around me, you men of Faith, and listen to the Word. I aim to show you what the Faith in the Word will do. It will lift mountains. It will put life back into the dead bodies on this hill here tonight. Here are the dead beneath these weeds and the dead leaves. And one of these dead shall breathe the breath of life before mornin. Brother Sluss, get up off the ground and go right out there to that chimney butt, look under the jam rock where the pothooks used to swing and bring me that coal pick, that corn scoop and that long-handled shovel."

"Where did you say to go, Brother Groan?"

"Out there and look in the butt of that chimney."

"Out there by the blackberry briars, Brother Groan? I'm worked up with the sperit."

"What are you goin to do, Brother Groan?"

"Through me, Brother Redfern, God is goin to give new life to a dead woman this very night."

"Who, Brother Groan?"

"My dead wife."

"Your wife!"

"Yes, my dead wife. What do you think I brought this

bundle of clothes along for? They are the old clothes she left in the shack when she died. She is goin to walk off this hill tonight with me. She is goin to live again through the Faith in the Word. It will put new life into the dead. It will lift mountains. You see, Brother Sluss come here with me a year ago today when my wife was buried here on this hill. You remember my wife, don't you, Brother Sluss?"

"Yes, I remember your wife. I was by her bedside prayin when she died. I heard her last breath sizzle. I heard her say, 'I see the blessed Saviour.' Then she was gone. I followed Joe Mangle's mules that pulled her here that muddy September day last year. When your wife died, I thought I'd have to die too. I just couldn't hardly stand it. You had a good woman."

"That cold rainy day was the day I waited till they had all gone off'n the hill but the gravediggers. And when they was throwin over her some of the last dirt, I watched them from behind the butt of that old chimney there in the blackberry vines—I was scrounched down there in that hole where the pothooks used to swing. And when one of the gravediggers said: 'Boys, since we're so nearly done and the weather's so rainy and cold, what's you fellars say let's slip down yander behind the bank and take a drink of licker? Looks purty bad to drink here over this woman's dead body and her a woman of God's, but a little licker won't go a bit bad now.' And they all throwed their shovels and picks down and took off over the bank. While they was down over the bank, I slipped out beside the grave and took a long-handled shovel, a corn scoop and a coal pick— I had this in mind when I hid, if they ever left their tools.

I wanted to see them throw the dirt in and I didn't want them to see me. I hid the tools in the butt of the chimney where I was hidin. And I said to myself, 'I'll come back here a year from today and I'll put new breath in her through the Faith in the Word.' So, I got the tools. I hid them right here. I stayed with them. The boys couldn't find their tools and they argued how funny it was their tools disappeared so suddenly, said it was such a strange thing. Some men accused the other men of not bringin their tools. They throwed in the rest of the dirt on my dead wife, then they swaggered full of licker off'n the hill. A red leaf stuck to the long-handle shovel handle. I think it was a leaf blowed off'n that sweet-gum tree right over there. There was death in that leaf, same as there was death in my wife. Dead leaves are on the ground tonight, not red with death so much as they was red with death last September in the rain when my wife was buried here."

"Brother Groan, I knowed your wife. She was a fine women, wasn't she."

"Yes. My wife was a very fine woman."

"Brother Groan, I knowed your wife since you spoke about her. Your wife had a harelip, didn't she? She was marked with a rabbit, wasn't she?"

"Yes, Brother Redfern, my wife had a harelip. But she wasn't marked with no rabbit. God put it there for the sins of her people. And my wife wouldn't let no doctor sew it up. My wife would say in church, 'God put this harelip on me for the sins of my people and I shall wear it for God.' My wife was a good woman."

"Brother Groan, I remember the woman with the harelip. And she was your wife! Well, I saw her five summers ago, a tall woman, slim as a bean pole, with a harelip. I saw her in Puddle, West Virginia. She was in God's house and she said the words you said that she always said about her lip. And one thing she said has always stuck with me. It was somethin like this: 'A man swimmed out in the river with his two sons. He was a good swimmer and they tried to follow him. He led the way for them. One went under the water and never come up again. The father started back with his other son toward the river bank and under he went too, never to come up again. 'My God Almighty,' the father cried out, 'my sons are lost. They went the wrong way too far and I led them. I led them into this danger.' And your wife fairly preached there that night. And the sperit of God was there in that house."

"Brother Groan, I was in Venom, Kentucky, two summers ago and I saw your wife. She was in God's house there. She had a harelip, I remember, and all her teeth nearly showed in front. They looked like awful long teeth. I remember when she was talkin to God she had a awful hard time sayin her words to God. She got up and said the words you said she said about her lip to the people, then she pulled her sleeve up and showed where she was marked on the arm by the belly of a sow. There was a patch of black sow-belly skin on her arm and thin sow-belly hairs scattered all over it. And there was three small sow's teats about the size of a gilt sow's teats. And your wife said: 'People, God has marked me because my people have sinned against God and I am to carry the marks of my sinnin people. I aim to carry the marks too. No doctor can cut the one off'n my arm or sew the one up on my lip.' Brother Groan, your wife was a good woman."

"Yes, Brother Littlejohn, my wife was a good woman."

"Brother Groan, I remember your wife. I saw her in God's house. It has been three years ago this September. I saw her at a tent meetin at Beaverleg, Ohio. And I'll die rememberin one good thing I heard your wife get up and say. She said: 'Women, if I had a man mean as the very Devil, which I ain't got, I would get up and cook for him at the blackest midnight. I would get a good warm meal for him if I had the grub to cook for him. Why? Because where he is goin after he leaves this world—there he won't have no sweet wife to cook for him.' Yes, I remember your wife sayin these words. She had a hard time speakin her testimony to God, for her words was not plain. I remember your wife and the half words she said. It was September in a hayfield near Beaverleg, Ohio, where the tent of God was. Your wife was a good woman, wasn't she?"

"Yes, my wife was a good woman, Brother Pigg. She was a good woman. You are goin to see my wife again. She is goin to walk off this hill with me. You bring the corn scoop here and shovel down through the loose dirt on top of the grave far down as you can shovel and lift out with the short-handle corn scoop. Here is the place. Start right here. Here is the place my wife was buried a year ago today. Yes, my wife was a good woman."

"Did you say to begin here, Brother Groan?"

"Yes, begin right there."

"Right at her feet?"

"I don't like to do this—mess with the dead."

"Ain't you got no Faith?"

[77]

"Faith in what?"

"Faith in the Word?"

"Yes, I got Faith in the Word."

"Dig then!"

"Well."

The moist September grave dirt is scooped out like loose corn out of a wagon bed. When the scoops of dirt hit the dirt pile, they are like so many dish rags hittin the kitchen floor. Dirt hits the dead weeds and the dead leaves on the ground in little thuds. The big moon is yellow above the dead dirty grass and the white tombstones and the rain-cloud gray tombstones. The disciples are silent now except for the wet dirt piece-meal hitting the ground. Brother Fain Groan is whisperin to God.

"I need the long-handle shovel!"

"Here is the shovel, Brother Pigg. Leave me dig a little while, Brother Pigg. Ain't you about fagged out?"

"Brother Littlejohn, I believe I will let you spell me a little."

"You have sure scooped this down some, Brother Pigg."

"I raised enough sweat. Closed in down here and the wind don't hit you right."

"Wind can't hit a body down in this hole, can it?"

"No."

"Boys, I'll know my wife by her lip. Thank God, I ain't ashamed of it neither. She told the people she wasn't ashamed of it. And I ain't ashamed of it neither, thank God. God don't heal this old clay temple of ours only through the Faith in the Word. I'll put breath back in my dead wife's body and she'll become my livin wife again. My wife—you have seen my wife and you'll know my wife when she is risen from the grave, Brother Sluss, and breathes the breath of life again."

Brother Groan walks out among the graves. His face is turned toward the stars. He whispers unknown syllables to the wind. The wind whispers unknown syllables to the weeds and to the dead leaves.

"I thought I heard a voice."

"A voice!"

"Yes."

"Ah!"

"The voice of God."

"No."

"It was the voice of the wind."

"Yes."

"The wind."

"The wind in the dead grass."

"Well then, did you hear the voice?"

"No."

"What did you hear?"

"I heard the wind in the grass."

"The wind!"

"Yes. The wind. The wind."

"You are gettin way down there, Brother Littlejohn. Let me spell you a little while with that shovel."

"All right, Brother Redfern. The ground is gettin hard here. Bring the coal pick down with you."

"Did you know there is a slip on one side of this grave? There is a hole down in this grave like a water seep. That is what made the shovelin easy. That is why we are gettin along fast."

"Is it?"

"Yes."

"Throw me down the pick, Brother Pigg. I have found some white tangled roots down here. Wait! I may be able to pull them out with my hand. A root this big, down this far in the ground—I don't see any close trees—it must have come from that wild-cherry standin over there on this side of the blackberry patch."

"Can you yank them roots out with your hands or do you want the coal pick? The ax end of the coal pick will cut them."

"Wait! I'm stung. The root flew up and hit my arm. Wait! Stung again. Wait! Here it comes. May be a snake! My God Almighty, but I'm stung. It can't be a snake though—a snake this deep down!"

"I'll see if it is a root. If it is a wild-cherry root it is a chubby wild-cherry root nearly as big as a two-year-old baby's thigh. My God, but it has stung me. It jumped and stung me. I am bit by a snake and you are bit by a snake. Yes. It is a snake. Strike a match! Watch—it is goin to strike again. Watch out. There! See it strike. It is a rusty-mouth grave copperhead. My God!"

"Come out of the grave, Brother Redfern. You have been bit by a rusty-mouth grave copperhead."

"Let us have Faith in the Word."

"Give me your pocketknife, Brother Littlejohn."

"What for?"

"To cut out the bite and suck the blood."

"Ain't you got no Faith in the Word?"

"Yes, but I know what to do for a copperhead bite. We ain't no business here messin with the dead nohow. It is against the Word to prank with the dead. Don't the Word

say, 'Let the dead rest. Bury the dead and let them rest'?
Give me that knife."

"Brother Redfern, I'll cut your arm on the copperhead
bite and suck your blood and you cut my arm on the copperhead bites and suck my blood."

"All right."

"God, ain't this awful out here this night."

"Brother Pigg is bit. Brother Redfern is bit."

"Go down in the grave, Brother Shinliver."

"Are you afraid to go? We're bit and we can't go back.
We're goin to get sick in a few minutes."

"I thought I heard a voice."

"You did."

"Yes. Is it God's voice?"

"No. It is the voice of Brother Groan."

"See him! He has opened the bundle of clothes he
brought. He is holdin up a woman's dress he brought in
the bundle of clothes he carried up here on the hill tonight. He brought them clothes to dress his wife in when
we get her dug out'n the grave."

"New clothes?"

"I'll ask and see."

"No—the clothes she used to wear. The dress Brother
Groan liked to see her wear. The dress she looked so pretty
in. Here is the hat she wore. It is a high-crowned black
hat with a goose plume on the side. And here are the
shoes she wore last. They are peaked-toe, patent-leather,
low-heeled, button shoes. The clothes are right here for
the woman soon as she comes out of the grave and the
breath of life goes into her lungs."

"I have hit the wood, men. It is the box. I'll have to

shovel the dirt from around the box so we can lift it out. I need hand holts. Wait till I clear some of the dirt away with my hands. I'm stung—stung like a red wasper stings right in the calf of the leg. Its teeth are hung in my pants leg. Get me out, men—get me out quick—it is another copperhead."

"Leave him out of the grave, men. See it. It is a copperhead. Its fangs are hung in his pants leg. Hit it with the shovel handle. Cut it with a knife. Kill it!"

"Cut the calf of my leg, Brother Littlejohn, with your pocketknife and suck blood, for I can't get to my leg to suck the blood out and the blood won't come out fast enough unless it is sucked out."

"All right."

"Strike a match. It is a she-copperhead. Its head ain't as copper as the he-copperhead's. I thought it must be a she, for the old rusty-mouthed one was the he-copperhead."

"Ain't you got no Faith in the Word, Brother Shinliver?"

"Yes, but Brother Littlejohn, we ain't got no business messin with the dead. The Word says, 'We must bury the dead and bury them so deep and leave them alone.' Don't the Word say that? I don't want my leg rottin off. Cut my leg and suck the blood."

"All right."

"I got that copperhead."

"Strike a match."

"See how gray the belly is turned up. It looks like a poplar root."

"Are you afraid of that grave, Brother Littlejohn?"

"No, I ain't afraid of that grave."

"Get down and shovel awhile then."

"You want the coal pick?"

"Yes, the coal pick."

"God—God, I'm stung. The first pop out'n the box and I'm stung right on the soft part of the jaw. The sting was like the sting of a red wasper."

"You stung, Brother Littlejohn?"

"Stung! Yes! My God! Take it off! Take it off! Its fangs are fastened in my flesh. Take it off, men. Take it off!"

"Yank him out'n the hole, men. All right. Come, Brother Frazier."

"Cut that snake off with your pocketknife. Cut it through the middle and it'll let loose. I've heard they wouldn't let loose till it thundered, but cut its guts out with a knife and it'll let loose, I'll bet you a dollar."

"Wait, I'll get it. Got it. Feel its fangs leaving your jaw?"

"No. My jaw is numb."

"Cut his jaw, Brother Frazier, and suck the blood."

"All right."

"You're hit awful close the eye."

"Makes no difference. Cut the bite and suck out the blood."

"Let me down in that grave, I'll take that coffin out by myself. I ain't afraid of no copperhead. No grave copperhead can faze me."

And Brother Frazier, short and stocky two-hundred-and-fifty-pounder, goes down into the grave. He is a mountain of a man. He lifts one end of the box, coffin and dead woman; he lifts it from the gluey earth. He lifts one end out and puts it upon the grave. The other end of the box rests down in the hole.

Brother Pigg and Brother Redfern are gettin mighty sick. They were bitten by the first copperhead, the rusty-mouthed grave he-copperhead. Brother Redfern and Brother Pigg are down under the hill by the wire fence. They are wallowin on the weeds. They are sick enough to die. They have a very high fever, the arm of each man is swollen and numb. They do not know they are wallowing on the weeds in the graveyard. They know no more than the dead beneath them.

Brother Groan comes up with the button shoes, the dress with the white dots, the black high-crowned hat with the white goose plume. Brother Fain Groan does not have a screw driver to take the coffin out of the box and the woman out of the coffin that the mountain of a man Brother Frazier lifted out of the grave hole alone. Brother Fain Groan grabs the coal pick. The box boards fly off one by one—these water-soaked coffin box boards. They are all off. Here is the color of an autumn-seasoned beech-stump coffin, rather slim and long the coffin is—but Sister Groan was tall and slender as a bean pole, remember. Brother Groan doesn't have a screw driver and he puts the sharp end of the coal pick under the coffin lid and he heaves once—only a screak like the tearin off of old clapboards pinned down with rusty square-wire nails. Another heave and another heave, still another and another—off comes the lid.

"My God Almighty. My wife. My God! My wife! Oh my God, but it is my wife. Perfectly natural too! My God! Oh my God Almighty! My wife!" Brother Groan just wilts over like a tobacco leaf in the sun. He wilts beside his dead wife. She wilted one year ago. The whole night and the copperheads is nothin to him now. The night is neither dark nor light to him. He knows no more than the dead woman beside him.

"That's Groan's wife all right. See that lip, Brother Sluss."

"Yes, that is Brother Groan's wife all right. Strike a match. See that arm where it is crossed on her breast. That is Brother Groan's wife all right, Brother Frazier."

"She looks like a rotten black-oak stump since the wind hit her on the face, don't she?"

"She looked like a seasoned autumn-beech stump before the wind hit her face, didn't she?"

"Yes, she did."

"But she looks like a black-oak stump now."

"No. She looks like a wet piece of chestnut bark."

"Ain't it funny the things the wind can do. Change the looks of a person. Talk with God. Whisper around in the corn like Brother Groan whispers to God."

"What is that smells like wild onions in a cow pasture?"

"No, that smell to me is like the sour insides of a dead persimmon tree."

"Let's get away from here. Shake Brother Groan. Get him up and let's go."

"Brother Groan won't wake. See how hard I pull his coat collar. He don't breathe. His heart has quit beatin. Feel! Brother Groan, get up and let's leave here! He's dead, sure as the world. Brother Groan is dead! His breath is gone! Let's get out of here!"

"I tell you, it don't pay to tamper with the dead."

[85]

"The Word says the dead shall be at rest. They shall be buried deep enough not to be bothered by men plowin and jolt wagons goin over the tops of them and the cows pickin the grass from over them. The Word says the dead shall rest."

"I think I ruptured a kidney liftin that box out awhile ago by myself. No, it don't pay to tamper with the dead."

Brother Frazier and Brother Sluss walk away from the grave. Brother Frazier walks like a bear. He is a short, broad man. He has to squeeze between some of the tall tombstones. Brother Sluss does not have any trouble. Here is Brother Littlejohn wallowin in the graveyard. He tries to get up and he falls back. He acts like a chicken that has lost its head, but Brother Littlejohn has not lost his head; his head is big and swollen. He does not know any more than the dead beneath him. Here is Brother Shinliver. He lies with his swollen leg propped upon the grave. He, too, is dead, dead as the dead under the ground—dead as Brother Groan, dead as Brother Groan's wife. Brother Pigg and Brother Redfern are lyin lifeless now, lyin down beside the wire fence where one first comes into the graveyard. They were tryin to get home. They couldn't get through four strands of barb wire stretched across the wind. They know no more than the grass beneath them or the dead beneath them. There is vomit all around them on the grass and the dead and the half-dead weeds and the dead leaves. Brother Sluss and Brother Frazier leave the graveyard. They are afraid. They leave the dead there and the sick there with the dead. They go down through the peach orchard, the corn patch, the pig lot and the cow pasture. They are crossin the cow pasture now—down the path where the pawpaw bushes trim each side of the path. Brother Frazier says: "Brother Groan died beside of his dead wife. Or was that put-on, do you suppose? Was he in a trance or was he dead?"

"No, Brother Groan is dead. His heart stopped beatin and I suppose he is dead. I guess that kills the old clay temple when the heart stops beatin."

"I don't believe Brother Groan had the right kind of Faith in the Word."

"Let your wife die and be dead a year. Go at midnight and dig her up and look at her and let the moon shine down on them lip-uncovered front teeth of hers and see what it does to you. See if your heart beats. See the pure natural bloom on her face at first. Strike a match and see the wind turn it black right before your eyes while the match is still burnin and you'd forget all about the Faith in the Word."

"Yes, I saw that. I got sick too. I tell you it don't pay to dig up the dead. The Word says the dead shall have their rest. The Word says the dead die to rest, that they shall be buried deep enough to get their rest without bein bothered by cattle pickin grass from over them, wagons makin tracks over them, men walkin over them. Then we go out and dig up Brother Groan's wife. It is the Word that filled that grave with copperheads. The copperheads was put in there for a purpose when Brother Groan hid in that chimney butt and hid them tools in there that he stole from the grave diggers. We have worked against the Word."

"I got awful sick there at the grave when the coffin was opened and I saw Groan's wife. Lord, I got sick when I saw that mark on her arm—looked plain-blank like the

[87]

belly of a young sow. I saw the lip too—a three-cornered lip and it black as a last year's corn shuck. It had long white teeth beneath it and one could see the roots of her front teeth. And then her face was the color of a rotten stump. I saw the face turn black as the match stem burned up in the wind. Lord, I had to leave."

"It wasn't the looks that made me sick. It was that awful scent when the coffin was opened. I smelled somethin like mushrooms growin on an old log—a old sour log where the white-bellied water dogs sleep beneath the bark."

"Smelled like wild onions to me."

"I don't believe that Brother Groan had the right kind of Faith. I have never thought it since we was all supposed to meet down there at the Manse Wiffard Gap at that sycamore tree. We was to crucify Brother Groan that night. We was to tie him with a rope to a sycamore limb. And he said his sperit would ride to Heaven right before us on a big white cloud. We went down there and waited around nearly all the night and he never did come. I don't believe he had the right kind of Faith in the Word."

The sun is up. The bright rays of sun, semi-golden, fall on the peach-tree leaves. The oak leaves swirl like clusters of blackbirds in the wind—red, golden, scarlet—semi-golden oak leaves the color of the one that stuck to the shovel handle last September. There is fire in the new September day. The wind is crisp to breathe. The tombstones gleam in the sun; the wind has dried the dew off the weeds, the wind has dried and half-dried the vomit on the leaves and on the grass and the vomit that still sticks to the lips of the four senseless yet livin men that lie in the grave-yard with the dead.

The neighborhood is astir. They hunt for Fain Groan, Wilkes Redfern, Roch Shinliver, Cy Pigg, Lucas Littlejohn; David Sluss and Elijah Frazier could tell where they are, but they are ashamed. They slipped in at their back doors. They are in bed now sleepin soundly as the dead.

People know here in the neighborhood that Fain Groan has a band of disciples, that they meet two and three times each week in the woods and in old houses; but they have always come in before daylight. The neighborhood is astir.

But Constable Ricks sees somethin from his house. He sees something goin on up at the graveyard. He has seen plenty of buzzards and crows workin on the carcasses of dead horses, but he has never seen such a swarm in all his life as he now sees upon the hill at the graveyard. He sees crows sittin up in the wild-cherry tree—enough of them sittin upon the limbs to break them off. There are the guard crows even. The ground is black with crows. He hears the crows caw-cawin to each other and to the buzzards tryin to fight them back. But they are turkey buzzards and they won't be whipped by cornfield crows. They fluff their wing feathers and their neck feathers right out and, like fightin game roosters, take right after the crows. The crows give back when they see the turkey buzzards comin. They don't give back until then. Crows fly from the ground up into the wild-cherry tree and then back to the ground. They change about, crow-habit; some guard while others eat.

Constable Ricks starts for the Kale Nelson Graveyard. He is ridin a mule. He lopes the mule up the hill. He sees a pile of fresh dirt before he gets there, he sees somethin like a box on top of the ground, somethin like a man, somethin like a pile of clothes. Up to the graveyard and he sees. The crows fly up in a black cloud. The buzzards are very slow about it, but they fly up too. He ties the mule to a fence post. One buzzard alights on the back of the mule and scares him. Constable Ricks rides the mule back fast as the mule can gallop to Coroner Stone's house and calls him from the corn patch. Coroner Stone jumps on the mule behind Constable Ricks. They gallop the mule back to the graveyard. Here are all the crows and buzzards back and more are comin.

When they scare the crows and the buzzards off Brother Groan and Brother Groan's wife, they fly down at the lower end of the graveyard, they fly down to somethin on the ground. Many as can find a place to light on the fence posts. Constable Ricks runs down there and shoos them away and strikes the air at them as they fly with the long-handle shovel he picks up back at the grave. He finds four men on the ground and finds plenty of sun-dried vomit on the leaves and on the dead weeds. Wilkes Redfern, Roch Shinliver, Cy Pigg, Lucas Littlejohn are lyin senseless on the ground. Constable Ricks thinks they are dead the way the crows are tryin to get to them and the way the buzzards are fightin back the crows from them. He goes up and feels over each heart to see if it is beatin. All hearts are beatin. The flesh of each man is cold. The warm September sun has not thoroughly thawed them after the cool night. "Found four men senseless but yet alive, Fred. Come down here. Let's take care of the livin first." Constable Ricks picks up a clod of dirt and he throws it at the crows with intent to kill. The clod goes through the whole flock of crows and does not touch a feather.

• Word and the Flesh •

Coroner Fred Stone stays with the dead and livin at the
graveyard while Constable Ricks jumps on the mule and
gallops over the neighborhood to tell that he has found
the missin men. Coroner Stone finds the rusty-mouthed copperhead, the she-copperhead and the young copperhead.
The snakes are dead, wilted and limber like a dead horse-
weed in the sun. He knows the four men have been bitten
by copperheads down under the hill by the wire fence
where one first comes in the graveyard when walkin up the
path, and not ridin a mule or bringin a team. He looks
at the face of Brother Groan; it is black—black as a wilted
pawpaw leaf. It has been picked on by the crows. But
picked on is all. His face is old and tough. It is tough as
crow meat. Brother Groan's wife's face is the color of a
young blackberry sprout hit by a heavy October frost—
wilted and soggy black. Her face has been picked on by
the crows. Most of it is gone. Coroner Stone looks carefully at the dress with the white dots, the patent-leather
low-heeled button shoes, the black high-crowned hat with
the white goose plume in the side. They are in Brother
Groan's left arm, his arm is wound around them like the
short stubby body of a copperhead and his dead fingers
clutch them like copperhead's fangs. Before the neighborhood gets back upon the hill and Constable Ricks comes
with the spring wagon to haul the four senseless men
home, Coroner Stone holds his inquest: "Fain Groan com-
mitted suicide when he dug his wife up and looked at her."
He said: "I know he planned to dig her up because here
are the old clothes I used to see her wear." That was Coroner Stone's duty.

When Constable Ricks comes upon the hill he arrests

the dead man. He thinks that is his duty, for he doesn't know much about the Law. He arrests him on the charge of "Public Indecency." Then he says: "My duties have been faithfully performed within the 'sharp eyes' of the Law."

The neighborhood men put Fain Groan's wife back in the coffin and give her a second burial. They hang the copperheads on the fence wires, for they say it is a sign of rain to hang a dead snake on the fence. They throw the four men in the wagon, senseless but livin men—throw them in like four barrels of salt, throw in Brother Groan with his loose flowin robe like he was a shock of fodder with loose stalks danglin around the edges, and they hurry them off the hill in the spring wagon.

Quinn Snodgrass claims the body of Fain Groan. Fidas Campbell claims him too. Quinn Snodgrass is the brother of Fain Groan's second wife; Fidas Campbell is the brother of Fain Groan's first wife. His third wife didn't have a brother to claim him as it is the custom to be buried by the first wife and that is in keepin in accordance with the Word. But Quinn Snodgrass got the body of Fain Groan.

It was the first house beside the wagon road and the team pulled up and they carried his body in the house, though his dead body was still under arrest for Public Indecency. That day Quinn shaved the long beard from Fain Groan's face and cut his hair. He pulled the Christlike robe from his body and bathed his body in water heated in the wash kettle, put the moth-eaten minister's suit on him and prepared him for a nice clean burial. Out in the cow shed, hammers and handsaws were kept busy all the

time makin his coffin. The next mornin he was hauled in
a jolt wagon, with four boys a-sittin on his coffin, to Pine
Hill Graveyard and buried beside of his second wife, Sy-
manthia Snodgrass. He was still under arrest for Public
Indecency for diggin up his wife so the crows and the buzzards could expose her parts.

There was a quarrel between Beadie Redfern and Sibbie
Frazier over Fain Groan's wife's clothes that were picked
up at the grave upon the hill. Sibbie got the hat and shoes
and Beadie got the dress. Men came and claimed the tools
and thanked whoever found them. Tim Holmes claimed
the long-handle shovel. Carlos Shelton claimed the corn
scoop. Bridge Sombers claimed the coal pick. All testified
they had been missin since the day they buried Fain
Groan's wife the first time, a year ago the day before.

It is tough now to see Cy Pigg and Wilkes Redfern
tryin to plow with one arm. Looks like together they would
make a good plowin team. Wilkes lost his left arm. Cy
lost his right arm. It is horrible to watch Lucas Littlejohn
tryin to eat with just one jaw. One can see his teeth grind
the food and watch some of it squirm out through the
hole in his jaw if one wants to watch it. The doctors
couldn't keep the flesh from rottin and fallin out, though
pokeberry roots and sweet milk did heal him. And there is
Roch Shinliver, fat as mud, hobblin around on a wooden
leg. People knows his tracks by a big shoe track and a peg
hole in the ground. His leg is all there—the bone is there;
it has never been taken off where the flesh rotted from the
copperhead bite and the muscles rotted and left the white
bone.

VIII

Disputing Warriors

ᕫ§|| We had driven back to our land of the
sky on Seaton Ridge to pick more huckleberries, when I
walked across the alfalfa to our old sheep barn. I wanted
to see if the high winds had blown the barn doors open
again. I wanted to see how everything looked inside the
barn, too, since Hubert and I had cleaned this barn
months ago. I opened the small door and started through
the stalls on the east side. I stopped at a pile of tobacco
sticks and picked up one. I thought I might need a stick.
Then I walked over about midway of the barn and here I
stopped suddenly. It was through that inner sense of cau-
tion, given a man for his own protection, that I stopped.
For here lay a big, fine-looking, bull blacksnake.

"So, old fellow, you've crawled inside the barn to get
cool," I said, drawing my tobacco stick up over my head.
I planned to let him have it. "You blacksnakes just won't
stay out of this barn. You must believe there are birds in
here."

Something kept me from coming down on this beautiful
snake with my tobacco stick. I knew he had come inside
this barn for a purpose. I thought that purpose was to
get himself out of the hot sun and to crawl over the
soft barn floor, which was a treat to his soft under-belly.
He'd been crawling over the stones, briers, grass and the

rough earth. This barn was a paradise for him. I brought my tobacco stick down easy and leaned on it as if it were a cane. I looked the big bull blacksnake over. He looked at me, too, with his black little beady eyes. He was a friendly big fellow. His being friendly paid off for him, for I still held my tobacco stick, a deadly weapon for snakes, in my hands. But old bull blacksnake didn't even offer to crawl away.

There wasn't a bird's nest anywhere. So I was positive he hadn't come for a mess of young birds. However, I felt he had come to this barn for some purpose. But he didn't coil to strike me. I didn't offer to hit him. He seemed to say: "Let's be friendly this time." And I was willing to be friendly with him. The larger the blacksnake, usually the friendlier one is. Never will a blacksnake attack a person. Never will one bite a person unless hemmed in and made to fight for his life. Then one's bite is harmless. "You're too pretty to kill," I told him. "I'm going to leave you." So I walked on.

I hadn't walked ten feet until I looked under the manger and here lay coiled, ready for action, a beautiful copperhead. He was short, thick and powerful. His tail was so blunt, I thought it might have been chopped off with a hoe once on a time. But a blunt tail is the true mark of a copperhead. He was the color of an old copper penny. I knew here lay a dangerous snake and I gripped my tobacco stick. I was ready for action if this snake even pretended to move. I thought he was waiting for me to take another step so he could let me have his fangs in my leg. But I didn't take the other step.

Now I knew why bull blacksnake was in this barn. I

knew he had come for a reason. Now I knew what that reason was. Only a few feet separated him and his greatest enemy. I wondered if he had smelled this copperhead. I wondered why he had followed through to spearhead his attack! Could he smell the copperhead like a human being with a good nose can smell one? One smells like cucumbers on a hot day. A person can hardly miss the smell of a copperhead.

I had planned to kill you, I thought, as I stood looking at this copperhead. I was still gripping my tobacco stick. But I am not going to kill you. I am going to leave you right where you are. So I relaxed the grip on my tobacco stick and I stepped back one step toward bull blacksnake. I stood between these reptile enemies. And I could have killed both of them. But I made up my mind not to do it now that I knew why bull blacksnake was in this barn. Had bull blacksnake not been here I would have killed the copperhead.

Somewhere, I thought, was old bull blacksnake's wife, a long female blacksnake. She was probably down under the ridge among the high cliffs. And somewhere she had deposited from ten to thirty eggs with soft tough shells in a hole in the loam. Perhaps she and old bull blacksnake were waiting for the hot sun to hatch these eggs. Maybe they'd already hatched and from ten to thirty little black-snakes were getting their soft under-bellies toughened up, crawling and playing over the rough land. But since this ridge land of tall yellow pines, sandstone cliffs and huckle-berry patches was the home of the copperheads, then the blacksnakes had fear for their young in this land of their enemies.

One of these young snakes, smaller in circumference than my little finger, wouldn't have much of a chance with a deadly copperhead—one lying in wait like the one under the manger. So, perhaps, old bull blacksnake was clearing this ridge land of his enemies which were my enemies, too. He was making this ridge country a safe place for his posterity. So I certainly wouldn't bother him now. I was so happy I hadn't bothered him. And I was happy I hadn't killed the copperhead. If bull blacksnake had tracked him down, if he had winded him in the air, this was his snake. He should be left alone for old bull blacksnake to kill. I would not interfere.

But while standing in this barn, another idea came to me. If and when the copperheads got too thick on this ridge, where we no longer let forest fires burn over every spring to kill them and destroy the timber as our people had once done, I had another idea for the elimination of the copperhead. If it were possible, I would order a barrel or more of blacksnakes and turn them loose on this ridge. Life, then, would be unbearable for the copperheads. In the question of survival between these two species of snakes, the one with the greater number would survive. And if one were to survive I favored the bull blacksnake. At least this was an idea. And why wouldn't it work?

Bull blacksnake among the huckleberry vines was harmless. He wouldn't bother anybody. He'd crawl away when he heard the huckleberry pickers' feet rattling the pine needles and their hands swishing among the huckleberry vines. He didn't want to bother a human being. One of us was not his enemy. In fact, he would become a very fine pet, if and when one took the pains to fondle him a bit and carry him around. He would like to be a pet, caressed and loved. But try to pet a copperhead and this was something else! Only a madman would do this! I was on blacksnake's side.

Since I had to be on my way to pick more huckleberries, I did one little thing before I left. I encouraged bull blacksnake with my tobacco stick to move over a little closer in the direction of the copperhead. He was hard to usher over. He went very cautiously and slowly. I didn't force him to go too far. I gave him a good chance to coil his long powerful body and to get ready for the fight that would soon come. I wanted him to fulfill his mission. I would have waited and looked on but it might have been an hour or so before the battle. I left these disputing warriors alone in my barn to battle it out for supremacy. I knew in advance who would be the winner. This was the only reason I had not used my tobacco stick.

IX

Time of the Cottonmouth Winds

❧‖ This was the right time to walk down the channel of the stream. Everywhere the land was dry and parched. There had not been rain for weeks. And across the long bottom where the yellow soybean leaves were dropping to the ground, gray soup-bean–colored clouds of dust arose. They swirled over and over, trying to catch each automobile.

Gray dust had settled over the strips of late-summer green, an acre in depth, along either side of this lane road. Dust had settled in the tops of trees sixty feet tall. Dust had sifted down among the soap-bellied leaves, making a preening sound when the dry cottonmouth winds blew. This was the right time for me to be hunting water. However, I didn't know why I was doing this. My curiosity compelled me to start down this dry creek channel in the midafternoon of this hot September day to see if there were any holes of water. This almost perpetual stream had ceased to flow for the first time in many years.

My shoes clicked against the bottom of the stream's channel on the rough rock floor. Dust arose in tiny clouds where I stepped. It was very strange to see dust coming from the bottom of the creek's channel. In the late winter when the snows melted on the high hills, streams of snow water came over high bluffs and walls of rocks to fill this deep channel to overflowing. My eyes were just even with the soybean bottom where I watched the yellow leaves dropping like rain while I smelled the dust that had blown from the lane road. Dust had settled on this soybean-gold, poplar-green, sourwood-purple, and sumac-red like a thin snow.

Somewhere there must be water in this stream, I thought. Somewhere, water must seep from springs under these high banks to make puddles where terrapins, squirrels, 'possums, rabbits, and foxes will find a place to drink. Even the snakes, I thought, must come to drink. They must have water the same as anything else.

I walked on, thinking what a rough deal life was for all the little creatures of the world. Man's greatest sport was to kill these creatures. And for their own survival they often caught and killed each other. Each one that walked, ran, or crawled had many enemies. And the birds had enemies in the air and on the land. Among the creatures of this earth, very few were friendly with each other. There wasn't much mutual trust among them. The old water-drinking terrapin had more friends than many of the others because he had a protective shell. He was a hard one to kill and difficult to devour.

Down in a portion of the channel, which centuries of surging waters had whetted lower than other parts of the stream bed, was a small damp place where the dust didn't rise when I put my foot down. Here the water had recently evaporated. But this had happened before a tired, old, thirsty terrapin had reached the place. He was lying here dead, his wrinkled bony face thrust to the hot wind. He had died of thirst. From a steep ledge, a ground squirrel ran out barking at me. I knew he had found water somewhere. Water had to be close. But a ground squirrel wasn't like a terrapin. He could travel faster and farther to find water.

Along the stream, the snakefeeders buzzed over. I wondered where they got water. Honeybees and bumblebees chased the soft fragile butterflies from the hot blossoms of phlox. The bees weighted these blossoms until the hot phlox stems reeled. Maybe they were drinking nectar as a substitute for water. Surely this wasn't true of the butterflies. They liked to drink water on hot sand bars where the creek water was bath-water warm. They visited the hot, wet sand bars along the stream in summer, like people who sat on stools in soda fountains. Somewhere, not too far away, was water. I walked on down the dry channel kicking up clouds of dust.

Around the next sharp turn, I met a terrapin walking toward me. He stopped, looked at me with his black, beady eyes, but didn't go back into his shell. There wasn't any need to. He must have detected I was a big friendly man. He walked slowly upstream, craning his neck once to look back. When he looked back, I was looking back, too. His beady, black eyes were shining in the sun like dark lumps of coal. A rabbit darted past me. Another ground squirrel gave a few low barks, scaled the high channel wall, ducked under the wilted bull grass, and was gone.

Across a dry sand bar I found the smooth, continuous tracks of snakes that crossed and crisscrossed like writing on the sand. Theirs was a language I couldn't decipher. I didn't attempt or care to decipher it. Water was close. Around another bend, I found water. Here the stream had dropped over a stratum of dark hard rock which was the color of pig iron. This rock had withstood centuries of flowing water. It hadn't worn away like other strata below. There was a deep bowl where water had once poured over. Now this bowl was filled with water, like some iron vessel entrenched in solid earth.

This pool of water didn't have a good smell down in this sultry hot afternoon world under the high channel banks. Streams of perspiration were running from my face. Why was I out doing this? What was I searching for? Well, I didn't exactly know. But man was curious where life was concerned. I'd thought of so many things on earth that needed to drink in this time of drouth. How do the living things find water? I thought. Where do they come from? Do they get thirsty like people? Will they fight over this water hole? I'll see.

I sat down on the dry bank just across the channel from the water hole. The sun was high enough for its rays to drop into the channel on the water. The steep bank on the western side of the channel couldn't obscure the sun's rays. Not yet. And the pods of wilted locust leaves hanging above kept the sun from beating down on me. I had a seat on the hard dry ground near the water hole where I could see everything.

I saw one minnow in the water hole. He seemed greatly disturbed. He swam the length and breadth of this hole, six by four feet, a half dozen times. When a little ground squirrel came to the hole to drink, this minnow saw its shadow. He swam faster than ever in his small decreasing world. He couldn't go upstream, or down. He didn't have the range he once had. He was the only occupant of this small pool of warm, stagnant water. The butterflies sat back a few inches from the water's edge to drink from the soft sand. How much longer will this water last, I thought.

While the ground squirrel was drinking, he looked up-stream and saw me sitting under the locusts. He gave a shrill bark and leaped across the sand toward the butter-flies which, frightened, rose like a bright cloud on their air-light wings. The butterflies' soft, fragile wings bounced on the waves of heat as they scattered in all directions. They fluttered in the heat scarcely a minute until they descended to their fountain of sand, where they settled down for more warm drinks.

When the shadows from their wings fell onto the little pool, the lone minnow swam for his life. He raced forward, around, and across, for in all directions he was faced with walls of stone. He was a lonely streak of living silver, ap-proximately three and a half inches long. He had once be-longed to a family. But where were they?

Once this minnow and the family to which he belonged swam lazily in a clear pool of fresh water, waiting for a fly or a bug to drop down from the willow leaves. When one fell onto the water, all raced to be the first there to get it! And they could swim upstream or race down. Their world was without such limitations! I had these thoughts while I watched this lonely minnow. He jumped in the water when the shadows of butterfly and snake-feeder wings left a fleeting shadow upon the pool.

Then I heard a rustle on the dry stems under the wilted bull grass. I sat so still I stopped breathing when I saw the long water moccasin emerge from under this wilted canopy of grass. I wondered what he had been doing under there. Waiting for a ground squirrel, I thought. Maybe getting the last frogs sitting near this pool, catching the green flies that might have come here to drink. This snake didn't see me. I sat like a stone statue, holding my breath, under the locust with the pods of wilted leaves. I breathed a little of the dry cottonmouth wind so I wouldn't make any noise. My body was as motionless as the wilted pods of locust leaves hanging in the sun-filtered air. There were not any preening sounds of snow-dust slithering from the soap-bellied poplar leaves. I sat thirsty in the world of thirst where the minnow ran wild in his limited world and the big snake crawled toward him.

When the butterflies saw the snake coming across the sand, they rose in a brilliant cloud. The snake didn't intend to disturb the butterflies, but they didn't trust him. I didn't like his looks either, for his skin was almost the color of gray dust. But the snake knew where he was going, all right. He had some purpose in his traveling. He was going to the hole of water to get a drink. He put his head down into the water, diving down like a long submarine. Then, I saw something else. He'd not gone to get a drink. He had another purpose for going.

This long snake started chasing the minnow. He chased him around the pool, but the minnow was too fast. Then, I thought, he hadn't caught a frog or a ground squirrel. He was hungry. He had come for the last minnow. He had caught the other minnows in this family when they had come down the dwindling stream to their last little world. Minnow refugees were crowded in this small world when he found them. He had feasted here, since they couldn't go upstream or downstream to get away. They couldn't go beyond these rock walls.

This water snake chased the minnow until I was sure he had caught him. This didn't matter a great deal to me. Among these wild creatures, it was life preying upon life. Maybe this was the way it should be. The flapping and flopping of the big snake ceased, for the pool was stirred until the brown sand rose, discoloring the water. The water snake, I figured, had got the minnow all right. Since this was the last one, I shouldn't have let him do this. But I was lazy sitting under the locust shade in the sultry, dry-mouthed wind.

I kept my eyes glued on the pool. I breathed a bit easier now, for the snake was under water. He couldn't see me. But I knew he would have to rise. He couldn't stand the muddy water too long. Maybe it was the sand in the water that hurt his lidless eyes. He breathed air instead of water, too. He could stay under a long time without air, but still he had to come up. I watched for him. I thought about the times when I used to wait for a water snake to stick his head above the muddy water when I was a boy. I stood over the muddy pool with a stick. When he stuck his head up, I batted him over the head. I finished him off. This was the way I killed the water snakes. Now, I watched for the hard lips to come up first, then beady, black eyes that shone like lumps of coal in the heat of the white-hot sun.

There was a quiet lull. Then there was a ripple where the lips broke the muddy surface. Slowly, the hard bullet-like head came up with two shining eyes in the sweltering heat of the white sun. You feel satisfied now, I thought. You got the minnow. He didn't have a chance. I ought to have got up from here, found me a stick, and finished you when you crawled over the sand. A stick?

I started looking around for one. It was too late now, but when a snake was near it wasn't a bad idea to have a stick close. I located one about the length of a cane and approximately as thick as the small end of a baseball bat.

This stick was just across the channel, lying on the bank where a swollen stream had once deposited it.

After I'd found this stick, I looked back at the pool. The water was clearing. To my surprise, I saw what appeared to be a quick movement across the pool again. I watched closely to see. Again I thought I saw the quick movement like a bullet through water. This was the fastest movement I'd ever seen in a small pool of water. After the sediment dropped more, I saw the minnow. He was a silver streak in the partly-brown, sediment-colored water. The snake had tried to catch him, but he was too fast. The minnow was valiant. Here he was, in a little pool, with this big snake. In this small world, the snake had him hemmed in. After this chase, I wondered if he would try again.

Then the snake gave a great lunge through the water. Low sprays of sluggish water went up and fell back into the pool. The snake was off again. He must be very hungry, I thought. He hadn't found himself a more substantial meal of ground squirrel or a frog. He had come from under the bull grass to the pool to get this minnow. This second try was filled with great effort. A ground squirrel came, saw the commotion and the sand-stirred water. He turned tail, running fast as his little legs would take him. He dove back under the wilted bull grass, out of sight. He knew something was wrong. He probably knew what it was. He, too, might have reasons to fear this big snake. Maybe the snake had chased him under the shadows of the wilted bull grass.

How would I like to be in a cage with a tiger, I thought, as I listened to the slashing water. How would I like to be hemmed in with something five hundred times my size trying to swallow me? The two of us, my pursuer and me, locked in my small world beyond which was a world devoid of oxygen. Would I stand up in my limited world to be devoured or would I fight back? I began to sympathize with the little minnow.

He was fighting for his survival while I sat under the locust and wondered if I would fight for mine. I had wondered many times if life was worth it. The little minnow, by instinct, even if he weren't a deep thinker, thought so. He had thrown off one attack. If he could only survive this second attack. I sat by watching his gallant fight for survival. But the minnow didn't have a chance without me. If he could only survive until a rain filled this channel again!

The sun dipped under a black cloud that blew up from nowhere. A soft wind pressed against my flushed face. In the far distance, I heard a sound like a road crew dynamiting a cliff. But this was a distant sound. The sound that disturbed me now was the swishing water. I jumped up. I don't know why I did this. I grabbed the stick. I stood over this pool of muddy water. Suddenly the snake dropped his chase. This time he got the minnow, I thought. Surely he got anything so frightened and bewildered. I watched for his hard lips to come up. I waited and watched for a water snake like in the happy days of my youth.

Then, I saw the hard lips rise like a periscope. I held my club over my shoulder. When his head was two inches above the surface, I came over like striking at a ball. There was another flapping in the water. This time, a creamy substance like oily milk started spreading over the water hole. With the end of my club, I raked the big writhing snake out onto the bank. I had killed him all right. What more needed to be done to give him a quicker death with less misery, I did now. I beat him with the stick in this world of survival in which I had become involved because I felt deeply for the lone minnow. I was the minnow in the pool. This was my life, and my enemy was trying to take my only true possession. I didn't know I had liked life so well.

I had often thought that if somebody wanted to finish me off, I wouldn't fight for my life. I had often wondered if life were worth the effort, if countries were worth defending, or if it were better to surrender without firing a shot at the big enemy that wanted to gobble your little country up. All through history the large had devoured the small and the strong the weak. And yet, the little and the weak had fought back. I'd not seen any use in fighting against hopeless odds.

Standing above the pool, I no longer looked down on the dead snake on the sand. I watched the water as sediment dropped for the third time. I watched to see if I could see a little flash of silver as the whole heavens above me darkened and thunders roared. I hadn't deliberately wanted to kill this snake. I hadn't wanted to take sides or get excited, but I had.

I saw a silver flash in the sediment-tarnished water. The minnow had thrown off his enemy's third attack. And this enemy would never attack again. The minnow loved life. He hadn't given up. He was alive. The rain had begun to fall and I had to be going. A storm was coming that might fill this channel. The drouth had ended. Even the dust would be washed from the leaves. The time of the cottonmouth winds had ended.

X

The Usurper of Beauty Ridge

൵§|| When our "Beauty Ridge" Johnson roared down the Tygart River Road on his motorcycle with his hands up and his feet stuck out, one eyewitness thought he was pulling a stunt. "Beauty Ridge" could teach his young admirers and would-be competitors a few stunts in motorcycle riding, drag racing, and daredevil hot-rodding.

This time our "Beauty Ridge" Johnson was engaged in a different competition. The eyewitness who screamed with laughter as "Beauty Ridge" went by, leading the pack of cyclists, didn't see the big copperhead fighting "B.R." for possession of his flying cycle.

"Beauty Ridge" had cut tobacco all day, and at sundown he planned to get some fresher air by taking a spin down that wonderful road for motorcycles, State Route #2, which follows the Tygart River.

Near the Pine Grove School, he stopped to talk shop with admiring cyclists. "Beauty Ridge" was still warm from cutting the heavy burley, so he got off his warm cycle and walked a few steps away where his cronies rested under a tree.

While the proud owner of this motorcycle chatted away, a robust, conniving copperhead tried to take over. At this time of year, in cool September, when his mates were securely hibernated for winter, this old bull copperhead was out prowling for devilment. He might have thought he had found a nice warm place to hibernate, too. But he didn't know whose motorcycle he was climbing up in when he wrapped himself around a warm coil. The temperature was just right.

When "Beauty Ridge" was ready to leave his boon companions, the sun was down. The early September evening had chilled the motorcycle until the metal was cold. The old, cold-blooded copperhead was about to fall into a hibernation sleep.

But our young "Beauty Ridge" Johnson, a handsome, muscular, 225-pound, six-footer, who had never lost a fist fight or a race in his life, dropped into the seat, never suspecting a mortal enemy of man was hiding to deprive him of the machine he loved. He was away in seconds with the sparks and gravels flying.

When the loud-cackling engine warmed the coil, old copperhead awakened from his siesta. As "Beauty Ridge" opened the throttle, to bear down on the highway, the engine heat was unbearable for copperhead. He liked a temperature not too cold, and not too hot, but just right. Since "Beauty Ridge" didn't furnish him with a well-regulated, comfortable temperature, he reached out and bit "B.R.'s" leg up close where he sat on the plush, springy seat.

"Beauty Ridge" reported later he felt the terrible sting, like that of a sand hornet, but he didn't slow enough to see what it was. Such a thing as a sand hornet, wasp, hornet, or bumblebee sting had never fazed him. One of these little stings, so he said, never made him bat his eyes.

But the second sting, he reported later, was worse than

the first. He slowed and looked down. He put on the brakes in a hurry when he saw the usurper that was trying to take over. Before he could come to a dead stop, the copperhead had bitten him twice more, which made four times.

Our "Beauty Ridge" had never lost a fight or a race. And he wasn't going to lose this one. He came off his cycle in a hurry. Just as he cleared the seat, the old bull copperhead, madder than ever over the unregulated temperature, reached out half his length to bite "B.R." again.

By this time, "B.R." was more riled than the copperhead. With one hand he was going into his pocket for a knife so sharp and large he could cut the tobacco with it when his regular cutting knife failed, and with the other hand he grabbed the copperhead by the neck.

"Damn you," he said to the copperhead. "I'll choke your forked tongue out!"

He said a lot more he was too much of a gentleman to quote in the presence of his young admirers. But he choked the big, dangerous, bull copperhead's tongue out as he had promised.

"Now, I'll spit in your eyes before I carve you up," he told the deadly reptile.

So he spat twice, once for each of old copperhead's malicious, lidless eyes, before he pulled him from the coil and started slicing him into short lengths, beginning at his blunt tail and cutting fast up to his death-grip on the rusty, tough-skinned throat. Each slice that fell, he stomped into the dust with his heavy brogan shoe.

Making mincemeat of old bull copperhead and grinding that mincemeat into the dust didn't take a minute. But

now our young hill man, nice-mannered for the ridge
where he was birthed, cradled, and sprouted up into powerful manhood, wondered if the copperhead hadn't gotten
him, too, with four successful bites up near the seat of
his pants. One successful copperhead bite that high had
been fatal to many a hill man.

He took a lace from his briar-scratched brogan in a
hurry. He made a tourniquet and applied it between the
uppermost of the four bites and his heart.

"My leg is real big up there and full of muscles and the
lace would barely make it" he said later. "But I stretched
it to make the tourniquet work. I didn't want any more
blood pizened by that thing's bites to reach my heart than
could be helped."

Then "Beauty Ridge" cleaned the blade of his pocket
knife, which he had used on the copperhead, by sticking
it into his own good Tygart earth. After cleansing the
blade in clean earth, he sliced his own flesh over each of
the four bites. He let each gash bleed while he jumped on
his cycle and really opened the throttle until he reached
the hospital five miles away.

Due to his quick work, his fast thinking for his own
self-preservation, he is the only person known to survive
four copperhead bites that high on his body. He was only
in the hospital three days and now he is back on his motorcycle where he rides full speed ahead with his crutches
strapped on beside him. Our friend and fellow warrior
from our East Kentucky hills, "Beauty Ridge" Johnson,
doesn't give up easily.

XI

Death for Two

◆§|| Day before yesterday, when Gary Blevins was mowing our yard, he came running to the door and called to me, "Jesse, there is a copperhead out here." I got up from the typewriter and went to look. There lay the snake, lifeless, I thought, because there was no movement in its body.

"Whatever kind of snake it is, Gary, you have killed it with the lawnmower," I said. "And I don't believe it is a copperhead."

He had killed the snake all right. The rotary blades underneath the mower had killed it when the snake had, perhaps, raised its head. Still its head hadn't been severed from the body. The snake had a gray, light-brown and orange-colored body—a beautiful color with diamond-shapes outlined in dark markings. It was about three feet long. How could Nature design the coloring of a snake's body to be so attractive?

"No, it's not a copperhead, Gary," I said. "It doesn't have a blunt tail. Look what a pointed tail it has. And it doesn't have the brown-earth coloring of the copperhead."

"What kind of a snake is it?" he asked.

"It looks like what we used to call a house-snake," I replied. "I have never known the real name of this snake. I know it is harmless."

Now the snake was dead and Gary carried it across the road and buried it at the edge of the meadow.

Today, two days after this incident, when I came from the well with a bucket of water, I looked down on the very spot where Gary had killed the snake with the lawn-mower and here was another identical snake. I couldn't belive what I saw. First I wondered if Gary had carried the snake away and buried it. This had come so suddenly. Then I realized without doubt, he had taken the snake away—the one he killed—and buried it. I looked down at the snake and I was sure it was dead.

I took the bucket of water to the house and then I returned. I took a hoe, turned the snake over and got down on my knees on the grass to examine this snake. It was as dead as a snake could be. But there wasn't a mark—not one anywhere on the body of this snake. It was about the same length of the one that had been killed on this spot. The coloring designs of the two snakes were the same. These snakes undoubtedly were mates.

There was a saying I heard in my youth from my parents and others that if one killed a snake, within three days its mate would be found where it had been killed. We, my brother and I, were warned if and when we killed a copper-head, to be on the lookout for its mate on the same spot for three days. This we did, and often killed the copper-head's mate. But I had never known one to crawl up where its mate had been killed and die of grief.

This is what had evidently happened here. This snake had never been killed. It had died of grief for its dead mate. I picked up the snake on my hoe and carried it down to the edge of the meadow. I dug a small hole beside the scar where Gary had buried the one he had killed with a lawnmower. Here I buried this snake beside its mate, whose death had caused it to grieve itself to death. Here, the bodies of two snakes and their immortal love for each other were interred where meadow grass would conceal all, even to the little scar of their grave.

XII

The Blacksnake's Operation

～§‖ Jane and I were sitting at the picnic table in the back yard when we heard a noise like wind in autumn leaves.

A lean bullfrog was coming down like a bowling ball, down the steep slope from the peach orchard. Each time he hit the ground, a long blacksnake tried to grab him. I'd never seen a frog run for his life as fast as this one was running. Each time he hit the ground, I thought the snake would get him. But the frog would rise into the air faster than a June bug.

"Don't let it catch the frog, Daddy!" Jane cried.

The blacksnake didn't hear Jane's screams and my shouting and hand clapping. He was determined to get the frog. He was going to chase him all the way to the creek. Just as the frog reached the foot of the steep slope and started to hop across the little bottom to the creek bank, the blacksnake caught him.

"Come on, Jane!" I shouted. "Help me and we'll save the frog."

I started running for the log that lay across the little stream. Jane was at my heels. We crossed the broad, hewn log and turned to our left. In thirty seconds more we were beside the big snake, who was lying there in the grass, swallowing the frog. We saw the frog's hind feet go in just as we got there. When the blacksnake saw us, he started crawling slowly back toward the hill. But the frog inside him made a big hump on his long, trim body. And this big hump served as a brake and slowed him down.

When he started up the hill, he found a hole in the ground made by a mole. He stuck his head inside and crawled in up to the hump on his body. But this hump again served as a brake.

"You can't get away!" Jane cried.

I caught the snake by the tail and lifted him up. He was big enough to swallow the frog easily. And he would have enjoyed swallowing him if Jane and I hadn't disturbed him.

"The poor frog was trying to get back to his home among the water lilies," Jane said. "He wanted to get back and sing in the evening when the moon comes up! What are you going to do to that snake? Aren't you going to kill him?"

"Not if I can help it," I said.

The snake squirmed. I hoped he might lose the frog, but he didn't.

"But, Daddy, he's killed the frog," Jane said.

"No, he hasn't," I said. "Not yet."

"But the frog can't breathe," she protested.

"Frogs stay under water and do without air over a minute at a time," I said. "He's not dead yet."

I laid the squirming snake upon the close-cut grass in our yard. He was, like most blacksnakes, a big friendly fellow. He'd crawl away from a person any time. He didn't want any trouble with anybody. All he wanted was something to eat—a mouse, bird, frog, young rabbit, or a mole.

"Get me two forked sticks, Jane," I said. "Get them in

a hurry if you want to save the frog. You can find some up there where I scythed over the peach orchard."

"How big?" she asked.

"Big enough to fit over the snake's back and fasten to the ground," I said.

Jane ran up to the top of the steep bank, where there were many little bushes with good forks scattered over the ground.

Jane came running with the two forked sticks. I put one over the snake's body near his head. I pushed it down into the ground enough to hold him. Then I placed the other fork over the snake's body on the other side of the frog.

"We'll have to have another fork, Jane," I said. "We'll have to hold the rest of his body still. Get another fork in a hurry."

By the time Jane got another fork, I had my knife out of my pocket and had figured the right place to make the incision. I put the third fork over the snake to hold the rest of his body in line. I knew he would squirm when I went to work.

My knife blade was razor-sharp. I kept it that way for farm use. When I applied the sharp blade to his tough skin, the snake flinched. I'd seen so many snake skeletons on our farm that I knew a little about the blacksnake's anatomy. I knew I'd have to cut through his ribs to get to the frog. And I had to be careful not to cut the frog. He'd already had enough punishment. Jane stood by and watched me cut through the skin, then the ribs, and slowly now I opened the snake until she could see the frog. My incision was not big enough to get the frog through, so I had to make it longer.

In a matter of seconds, I got the frog by the hind feet

and carefully, slowly, I pulled him through the incision. I did as little harm to the snake as I could. He was squirming and Jane had to watch the forks carefully. Once he pushed the third one up, but Jane reset it. When I laid the frog on the close-cut grass stubble, he seemed lifeless.

"You're too late," Jane said. "The poor frog is dead."

"Maybe not," I said. "Go to the spigot and get some water and pour it over him."

Jane ran to the spigot and got a dipper of water. She poured the cool water slowly over the frog.

"He opened one eye," she shouted.

Soon the frog had both eyes open and was sitting up.

"He's going to be all right, Jane," I said. "Don't worry any more about the frog. But think of this poor, gentle blacksnake! He worked hard to get himself a meal. Now we've taken it away from him! We've got to save the snake!"

"Let 'im die, Daddy!" Jane said. "Snakes catch frogs, birds, rabbits, and moles! Snakes are killers!"

"So are frogs," I said. "So are birds and moles! They kill each other, plants, insects, flies, worms, and bugs. Each fights for survival. They play a great game. It is a rhythm in nature. They keep each other balanced. If it were not for the others, one would become a pest!"

"Not anything will kill a snake, Daddy!" she protested.

"Snakes kill each other," I said. "And chicken hawks, crows, and owls kill snakes."

Jane stood looking first at the frog, which was taking short, slow hops toward the stream. Then she looked at the incision in the writhing snake.

"You like the fireflies in the evening, don't you?" I said

to Jane. "You never run and catch them and put them in a bottle like other boys and girls. You say, 'I like to watch them light their own way through a dark night-world.' Well, the frogs sit down there on the water lily leaves and leap up and catch the fireflies when they turn on their lights in the dark night. That frog was up there in the peach orchard, wasn't he? He went up where there were plenty of green flies in the hot sunlight. He was up there getting his dinner and the snake was there hunting his."

"Well, what can we do now to save the snake?"

"Run to the house and ask your mother for the turpentine bottle," I said. "Then look in my tool box and get that roll of adhesive tape."

I had to set the forks deeper into the ground. The big blacksnake didn't like being held close against the ground so he could barely move.

When Jane returned, I put turpentine into the incision.

"Now, hold these forks down real tight, Jane," I said. "I want to do a good job!"

The snake writhed as if he were in much pain. I thought the turpentine might be smarting him. I unrolled the adhesive tape and cut several short strips in a hurry. Then I got down on my knees, fastened a piece of tape on one side of the incision, and drew the wound closed before I clamped the tape on the other side. I put tape on the incision from one end to the other. I had made this incision high enough so the tape wouldn't interfere with his crawling. I wanted to be sure I'd done a good job—one that would restore health to this big friendly snake so he could go into the ground after moles, mice, rats, and ground squirrels.

"Now take the forks up," I told Jane. "Let's see if he can't crawl away better than after he swallowed the frog."

Jane removed each fork and the big blacksnake crawled away very slowly at first. He held his head high in the air and stuck out his tongue.

"The frog got back to the creek and the snake is going back to the peach orchard," I said. "He's going back to live on his sunny south hillside."

"But why did we do all of this to save a snake?" Jane asked. "And, Daddy, come to think about it, after your telling me about the frogs catching my fireflies, I wonder why we saved the frog."

"They're both our friends, Jane," I said. "If it weren't for the frogs, I don't know what we'd do about bugs, flies, insects, and nests of yellow jackets. If it weren't for the blacksnakes, the moles would eat our garden. Blacksnakes catch mice, rats, and ground squirrels, and they kill the poisonous copperhead. They're friends to the farmers."

Our big blacksnake had reached the steep slope. He turned and looked back at us.

"I don't believe he holds anything against us, do you?" Jane asked.

XIII

Confrontation

❦|| There the old fellow lay, sprawled across the road, his sleek long body waved like a willow wand in the wind, but he held his head high. I brought my farm truck to a sudden stop, because I didn't want to crush his body and snuff out his life. He was a beautiful bull blacksnake, five to six feet in length. If I had driven five more feet, I would have crushed him against the white limestone gravels that covered the road.

"Wonder why he doesn't go on?" Naomi said. She was in the farm truck with me, and we were going to look at some oak clapboards we had riven to shingle the walls of our smokehouse. "Why does he just lie there and look up at us and lick out his tongue?"

"When he licks out his tongue, he is listening to what we are saying about him," I said. "His tongue intercepts the sounds of our voices. Say, he looks like Old Ben, that gentle old blacksnake we used to have at my home for a pet."

"You're not thinking about taking him for a pet?"

"I would like to have him all right," I said. "He'd make a good one. But I can't take him home because of our ground squirrels and young rabbits, our other pets. He'd go down in the little holes where the ground squirrels den, and he'd be an unwelcome visitor. If I didn't put him in a cage, he'd get my frogs, toads, and young rabbits, too."

"But you're not thinking about killing him?" she said, in a surprised tone of voice.

"Oh, no. If I had had such a thought, I would have run over him with that truck," I said. "I never crush a snake on the highway. I think it's cruel ... terrible."

Naomi wasn't listening to what I was saying. She was looking out at the window at his head. I was now looking out of my window at his tail. After I had seen him lying across the road, I had driven so close to him before I could stop, that the middle part of his body was hidden by the truck engine.

"He doesn't move," Naomi said. "Isn't he afraid?"

"Maybe the gravels on the road are rough for him to crawl over," I said. Then I stuck my head out the window and I shouted: "Move on so we can move, too!" But he just lay there stretched across the road. "Maybe you didn't hear me," I said. Then I honked my horn loud and long. "I know he can hear me now," I said, holding the horn down.

Then Naomi laughed real loud. "It's hard to believe you stop the truck for a blacksnake across the road, and honk the horn for him to crawl on, and he won't go. He's raised his head a little higher. And he's moving his tongue a little faster. I believe he is bewildered."

"I'll make him move on," I said.

"No, you stay in the truck and I'll get out and make him move," she said.

"You're not afraid of a blacksnake, are you?"

"Well, I'm not exactly friendly with one like you are,"

she said. "I never want one in my hands, but I can make him move."

She got out of the truck and she said: "Move on, Old Adam. You're in a dangerous place!"

"Say, Old Adam is a beautiful name for him," I said. "To his clan he might be the Old Adam. He's big, old, and beautiful."

She walked up closer to him. Then she said: "He won't move. There's not a stick around here that I can use to prod him. But I'll use my foot. I'll pretend I'm kicking at him."

She moved her foot in his direction. Then she laughed: "He drew his head back when I poked my toe at him."

"I'll make him move on," I said. "He's not trying to bite you, is he?"

"Oh, no," she replied. "But he doesn't seem to know I want him to get out of the road."

The big fellow had just come down from the slope of the high green hill. I could see his curved rope-like track on the sand where he had crossed the ditch to the road. "He's going to the creek to get himself a drink of water," I thought. There were no streams or springs that I knew of upon the steep slope where he could find water. Between the road and the creek there was a green strip of meadow about fifty feet wide. He was heading in the right direction to find water.

"The snake isn't considered to be a very smart species of life," I said, opening the truck door. "But snakes are smarter than we think. And the blacksnake is very smart!"

I got out and slammed the door behind me to scare the snake. The noise didn't scare him.

"I'll make him go," I said. "I'll get hold of his tail."

"Let's look at him first," Naomi said.

He seemed to be very contented lying stretched across this road. And he was almost as long as the road was wide.

"He's a nice-looking fellow," I said. "He's shed his old skin and his body is velvety smooth. I like the way he holds his head up high. He's got life and pride."

"But looks like he'd know enough to get out of the road," Naomi said.

"He'd make a wonderful pet," I said. "I'd really like to have him down at the house. But if I'd take him, then we wouldn't have any ground squirrels. So, we'll not take him with us. I believe he wants us to, though!"

"Well, one thing for sure, he's not afraid of us," Naomi said.

She poked her toe at his head again. He bent his long neck back in a lazy gesture. And now I looked at his beady black eyes shining in the sun. They looked like a ripe possum grape hanging on a leafless vine up in a leafless tree in late November.

"Well, I think he'd better move on," I said. "We've got to look at the boards."

I bent over and lifted up his tail. "Get going," I told him. "This road doesn't belong to you. Somebody will be less kind to you than we are if you don't get out of the road. Somebody might run over you with a car and think he's done the community a favor! And when he kills you, he will have killed a friend."

"I'll agree with what you say," Naomi said. "I know it's true. But I still can't exactly warm up to a snake."

Now his long body began to move in little zigzags as he

pulled himself slowly over the gravels. He took his time and when he bent his long neck to look back at us, he licked out his forked tongue. I thought he might be trying to thank us.

"Go on and get yourself a drink," Naomi said. "We are not going to hurt you. You'll find plenty of water over there in the creek."

Then she turned to me and said: "Wonder why people kill blacksnakes? Don't they know that if it weren't for the blacksnakes, we couldn't live here because of the copperheads?"

"No, they don't know it," I said. "And they don't bother to find out, either. People just feel sure any kind of a snake should be killed. Any kind of a snake is an enemy to them! And they also think the snakes kill too many birds. They don't consider how many birds are killed by owls and hawks for food. And man is the greatest killer of birds. Boys with air rifles and slingshots."

"Well, snakes do kill birds," she said.

"Snakes kill birds when they're hungry and can find a nest on the ground or up in a tree," I said. "After a snake finds food, he doesn't kill. The birds kill the moth, butterfly, and the worm. Snakes catch the birds. And crows kill the blacksnake. There is something to catch everything, but only a hog will kill and eat a copperhead. The hog won't eat a copperhead's head. How a hog, with as little sense as he has, knows a copperhead's head is poisonous has always puzzled me. Just about everything—reptile, animal, and bird—is afraid of a copperhead—everything but the blacksnake and the terrapin! But I wouldn't kill a blacksnake even if there were no danger of copperheads. And I certainly hate to see anybody kill a blacksnake in this copper-head country."

"You know, I was telling Mrs. Blevins the other day, we didn't kill blacksnakes, and she trembled and shuddered when I said 'snake'," Naomi said. "I believe she thinks we are a couple of eccentrics for saving them!"

We stood watching the beautiful bull blacksnake move slowly across the short grass in the meadow. He was holding his head high where he could see over the top of grass. His new, velvety-smooth skin was shining in the sun. The green meadow grass was a contrast to his long, dark body.

"The hornet and wasp snare the flies," I said. "And the spiders catch the flies in their webs, and the mud daubers fly in and catch the spiders. There is a balance in nature."

"Then we have vegetarians," Naomi said. "We have the rabbit, groundhog, muskrat, and the squirrel. These don't kill anything."

"But of all the predatory animals, birds, and reptiles that kill life to sustain their own life," I added, "our own species, man, is the greatest. This is the reason I have such great respect for the Buddhists. They don't kill. Wildlife in India is not afraid of man."

"Man and cats are our greatest killers," Naomi said.

"For fun, man kills animals he doesn't eat," I added.

"Look at the snake," Naomi said. "He's almost across the meadow."

He was holding his head barely above the green waves of grass that the lazy wind was slowly bending down and then easing up, to let the grass rise.

"The restless motion of the grass is like the restless motion of the green waves on the ocean," I thought. "The blacksnake's head is like the periscope of a submarine. . . ."

We watched the periscope submerge behind the bank into the channel where there was a clear, unpolluted running stream.

"We have a large flock of crows that feed in this area," I said to Naomi. We were back in the truck now. We were on our way to see the clapboards. "I hope the crows don't find our friend, for if they do, they'll pounce on him and have a great feast."

XIV

Old Jackson Was My Teacher

᠊ᡒ§|| If the President of the United States had asked me, before I had a heart attack, to come to Washington as fast as I could, I would have gone the fastest way. I would have gone by missile if I could. If the President of the United States were to ask me now, I'd go, but I'd choose my own way of travel, slow or fast, probably slow, the way in which I would be the most relaxed.

When my publishers send me proofs of one of my books they have had for a year, and they write they want the proofs back in a hurry, say three days from the time they reach me, they usually don't get the proofs back to meet the deadline. This gives me only a day to read the proofs on a book which has taken me, perhaps, a year to write. I have patience even if someone at the publishing house hasn't. I reason they have to have writers before they can be publishers. So why do all this rushing, which is not only contrary to my rhythm of life, but even contrary to their own rhythm of life. Patience is a key word to protect the heart, to keep hearts healthy that are already good, to prevent heart attacks and to soothe and help the weak and crippled hearts. And by using patience we can actually do more work than we can by rushing to meet deadlines.

I have never learned patience from any doctors. I have seen only one, in all my contacts, who isn't rushed until he doesn't have time to live. He is Dr. William Bray, the cardiologist I now see occasionally. All other doctors I have had and I know personally are rushed almost beyond human endurance, meeting deadlines and seeing more and more patients. How could one of these doctors have told me to use patience when it is an unheeded word in their own vocabularies? If they don't use patience themselves, how can they tell others to use it? Not one of them can ever say I learned patience from a doctor, for I haven't. I lived forty-six years of my life without patience. I was physically geared never to be a patient man. But after I had my heart attack, I had to acquire patience if I was to prolong my life.

And what if I were to tell one of my cardiologists or one of my medical friends how I came by it? I can see the expression that would come over his face. It would be one of joy. And he might even tell a joke of his own while he held the laughter so he could then explode into wild laughter, not at his own joke, but over my learning patience from a reptile. What living thing on this earth is more patient, and livingly gentle and in so many ways, than a blacksnake?

When I was a boy I thought the only good snake was a dead one. At my father's home I kept the hoe handy for any and all snakes. One lick with a sharp hoe and the snake was usually decapitated. My father was first to learn that a blacksnake was good on a farm, that it cleaned out the mice in the corncribs and haylofts and that it was a good rat exterminator. He would catch blacksnakes and bring them to the barn. But just as soon as a blacksnake crawled up a tree and fed on a nest of young birds, my father would use the hoe on all the blacksnakes he'd see for a month. Here his reasoning wasn't right. The blacksnake isn't the only predator of birds. Man kills more birds than the blacksnake, just for the joy of killing. What about a big man with a big gun snuffing out a quail's life while it's in flight, stilling its pinions and song forever, and calling this sport! How can the name "sportsman" ever be synonymous with killing? Quails have been killed until they are about ready to be relegated into antiquity like the passenger pigeon. The snake doesn't kill for fun. He kills for food.

When I really got to know the blacksnake was once in our pasture where I found a very large one coiled like a bundle of black rope. I had a stick ready to finish him. But he looked contented lying there. I think he must have been asleep when I first came upon him. Later he raised his head, licked out his forked tongue. I reached down and picked him up by the neck. He didn't want any fight with me. I measured him with my own body and he was six feet long. I took him home and put him in the corncrib. I named him Old Ben. At first my mother was afraid of him when she went to the corncrib to get corn for the chickens. He often would be asleep in the front part of the crib. Our dog, a great snake killer, tried to pull off parts of the crib with his teeth to get to him. But Old Ben soon won the affection of all members in our family and our dog that wanted to kill him. Children who came to play with my younger brother and youngest sister argued over who could wear Old Ben around his or her neck. My mother soon had no fear of him and she would pick him up with her hands when he got in her way and lay him aside. I've told the story before how Old Ben stayed with us two years.

In those days I was in my teens and as strong as an ox. I felt then that I would live forever! Old Ben was merely a pet, and my observations of him, which were affectionate ones, taught me to think twice before I ever killed another blacksnake. I never thought there would come the time when I would have to think back to this friendly old reptile and be an imitator of his patience to try to lengthen my life.

Then, luckily, something happened again to me just after I had learned to walk again and my fingers had lost their stiffness and I was permitted to use my typewriter. First year I was in bed and second year I was convalescing. And this event happened in the second year in the summer of my convalescing. I was out again in my old workroom, working at my typewriter. Above, on my bookshelf, on top of my books, a wren had built her nest. She had four baby birds she and her mate were feeding. And when they flew into the room with food, they flew not more than six or eight inches above my head. They knew I wouldn't bother them, that I was their friend. The wren had found a crack where the door had sprung, got into my workroom and built her nest before I got back to my room. Had I been able to go out sooner, I would have discouraged their building a nest on my books. Now they had built their nest and had young. If they had been afraid of me, I would have left the room until their young had grown up and flown away. But we got along all right together. They had no sense of fear of me.

But when a parent wren made a frightful noise, I looked over to the opened door and I saw a blacksnake's friendly face, crawling up the steps and licking out his tongue and looking at me with his black beady eyes.

"Come on in, Old Fellow," I invited the snake. He re-

minded me a lot of Old Ben. I was writing a story in which
I used the name Jackson. As he kept inching his long body
up the steps, I said: "Come on in, Old Jackson! Don't be
afraid."

And he came in. He was nearly six feet long. But here
he was in my writing room only a few feet from my chair.
Now the two parent wrens were flying in circles in the
room. They were fussing mightily. I thought they were
trying to tell me to do something with Old Jackson. And
I wondered if he had lain somewhere and had watched the
parent wrens flying in and out of my workroom and if he
hadn't figured there was a nest of young birds in here and
that he would come in and have a feast. The sense of direction of a blacksnake, who crawls on the ground and raises
his head above the grass like a submarine's periscope from
the sea, is something unusual. Once on Seaton Ridge at my
farm, I looked up to the top of a dead oak, a mere hulk of
a dead tree, sixty-feet-tall, without branches or bark, and
I saw a large blacksnake going into a hole that must have
been made by flickers. They had bored into the tree near
its top to make a nest where they thought their young
would be protected. How on earth did this blacksnake, so
low on the ground, ever find a nest this high in a tree unless he had coursed the parent birds to it? Now I had with
me in my room two parent wrens, four young wrens and I
had Old Jackson. I wondered if all eight of us couldn't re-
main in my workroom and if I couldn't discipline Old Jackson if he made toward the wrens' nest. He circled over the
floor, then came toward my writing table.

"Oh, no, Old Jackson," I scolded. "You're not going to
feed on these wrens! They are my friends too."

[137]

• Dawn of Remembered Spring •

I picked him up and carried him over to the far wall and put him upon the books in one of the shelves. I went back to writing my story. The parent wrens calmed down and began to feed their young again. But in a few minutes I heard a thump on the floor. Old Jackson had fallen off the books. He was large, awkward and clumsy. I stopped work and put him up again. I went back to work. Later I heard him fall again. I believed he was doing this on purpose and that he needed discipline. I went out into the yard, broke a small branch from the dogwood and came back to find him near my writing table, while the parent wrens were telling me to do something with him. I switched him enough to let him know not to bother the wrens. Then I picked him up and carried him outside into the yard. When I left this room, I closed the door. I looked at the little hole the wrens could go through and I knew Old Jackson could never get through such a small place. I felt satisfied to go away.

Thereafter, each morning at about nine, when I went to my room, it wouldn't be long until Old Jackson would come crawling in. He never attempted to bother the wrens again. He would lie on the floor where the morning sunlight filtered through the door. He seemed to enjoy the floor of my room for a bed to lie in the warm sunlight. He wanted to be my friend. When I told Naomi about what had happened, she said: "Jesse, I want you to get rid of that snake before he gets the wrens." But I didn't get rid of him. I was observing his patience. Always when I left my room, I put him out and closed the door so he couldn't get back when I was not there. I didn't trust him not wanting to feast on the young wrens. Then Old Jackson got to the place he'd follow me over the yard. He tried to follow me into the house. But this was something Naomi would never permit. Once she hit him lightly with a broom when he tried to follow me in.

Often when Naomi worked in the back yard, which seemed to be Old Jackson's much loved domain, she'd call to tell me to come and get him off the walk. If he couldn't lie in the sun on the floor in my writing room, the next best place was the walk. I'd go and take him from the walk, carry him over and put him on the grass. Later Naomi learned how she could get him off the walk so she wouldn't have to call me. She'd dash a dipper of cold water over him to make him move.

He became such a pest that I finally decided to take him away. I put him beside me on the seat of my pickup truck, hauled him down to the end of the lane road, which is two-tenths of a mile away, and turned him loose in the meadow. Next day he was back in our back yard. How could he remember the way I hauled him? I knew he was too low on the ground, even if he raised his head from the meadow grass like a periscope, to see where we lived. Yet he had come back. Second time I hauled him away, I took him two miles over to the bank of the Little Sandy River. Now the wrens had raised their young and they had flown from the nest. I was sorry Old Jackson had gotten so chummy, wanting to share our home with us, that I'd had to get rid of him.

He had been great company and a great consolation to me. In our back yard, I had observed many things about Old Jackson. Once when he was crawling up the bank behind my writing room, I noticed his long waving body was almost identical with the cardiograms the doctors had shown me of my heart. The heart had to beat for the cardiograph to trace its movements on paper. How could Old Jackson, by climbing up a steep bank, get his long body into this position? What was the symbolism I was discovering? I'm not a man too interested in symbolism, but I wondered how much or how little significance was here.

And many a time I found him lying with tip of tail touching his head in a perfect circle. Why would he, a lowly reptile, get into this position, when a circle is symbolic of so many things? The earth is round like a circle. The universe must be round. Certainly it is not square. And everything tries to work in circles. Life of man is a circle. In the beginning man is a child, and if he lives to be old, he performs in a circle and returns to childhood again. The canopy of sky above us on a clear day is a semi-circle. Stars and planets are round like circles. Birds make round nests. Hornets and mud daubers build round nests. The sun is round and during the day it performs in a semi-circle. It comes up in the morning and goes down in the evening. The moon is often a circle. Our four seasons here—spring, summer, autumn, winter and spring again—form a circle. We live in and by the power of the circle. Old Jackson, my friendly reptile, must have known instinctively of the circle's significance to life. At least he had reawakened me to return to the circle and to think about it. I had the circle in primary, secondary and higher mathematics but I wasn't as impressed with its significance then as I was now with my observations regarding its manifestations in nature and even in Old Jackson.

When I walked on the path to my writing room, Old

Jackson knew my steps and he came crawling. Since he had no ears, he caught the vibration of sound in his tongue. My steps were heavier than Naomi's. When he heard the sound of her lighter steps on the walk, he didn't come crawling. Maybe he would catch the swishing sounds of a bird's wings in flight by vibrations in his tongue. Don't we feel the vibrations of our beating hearts throughout our bodies? There is always that vibrant motion, always and always as long as we live. How much health knowledge could I gain from this patient, friendly blacksnake? Despite the unfortunate human curse upon him in a Christian world, he has managed by his own patience to survive. It is too bad that he was used as a symbol of evil with Adam and Eve in the Garden of Eden.

After my feeling kindly toward the blacksnake in my recuperative days (and so many local friends thought I was beginning to be a little strange on the subject), I learned more about the snake in my later travels to parts of the world where I had never been. Naomi, our daughter Jane and I went to live in Egypt for a year. Here Naomi taught children in the American School while I taught at American University in Cairo and Jane completed her freshman year at American University in Cairo. In Ancient Egypt I learned my observations about the blacksnake in America weren't new. Egyptians have no prejudices against the snake. The snake is regarded as a symbol of health now, as it was among the Pharaohs thirty-five hundred years ago when twenty-four pagan gods were worshipped. I was surprised at first to see the symbol of the snake on the gate of one old medical university. Chiseled from stone, wrapped around a gate post where one entered the university, was the snake. It was symbolic of medicine and health in the Land of the Pharaohs. It is still the symbol of medicine in modern Egypt. It is regarded as a symbol of goodness in the Valley of Kings. Here there is a very large mural, painted thirty-five hundred years ago and looking as fresh now as if it were completed last week, a painting of a huge snake carrying good people on his back from earth to paradise and spitting liquid fire at the evil ones who are trying to interfere with his going.

A year later when I was back in Egypt speaking at their colleges and universities under the auspices of the United States Information Service, which is called the right arm of our United States State Department, I gave four lectures at Alexandria University where the good Apostle Luke once taught medicine. And what did I see for four days when I entered and came from the University but the emblem of the snake on the gate.

In Iran, among those of Moslem and Zoroastrian faiths, there are no prejudices against the snake. In East and West Pakistan it was the same, except snakes and medical lore can hardly be separated. Here I told snake stories but I was always told better snake stories. It was here that people were afraid to kill a snake. And this is true among people of Hindu and Buddhist faiths. They do not kill snakes, no matter whether poisonous or non-poisonous. They have cults of snake worship. It is only in a Christian world where the snake is considered the lowliest of living creatures upon the earth.

If a living creature on this earth has some special significance that is of service to help me prolong my days that I may rejoice in being alive, be a part of the creativity, then there isn't any reason why I should not follow what is helpful to me. If this creature has mysterious symbolism of which ancient peoples approved and their modern descendants approve, why should not I, a man of the Western world and of another culture, approve?

But wouldn't it be funny in my country for friends to say I was following the cult of a snake? And what do you think our doctors would say? I have never heard one of whom I've been a patient ever say he liked a snake. Certainly never would one advise a convalescent to pace himself the way the patient blacksnake—symbolic of so much that is good in the world—does.

XV

A Thousand Years Is
a Long Time

~§‖ When I drove up to Ebbie Hopewell's farm house, there was a crowd of people standing under the sycamore shade in his front yard. I had come to see why Ebbie hadn't baled my hay yesterday. The radio predicted rain for tomorrow. I wanted to get the hay baled and stacked in the barn loft before the rains came. I wondered why Ebbie, whose word had always been good, hadn't come as he had promised. I parked my truck under the sycamore shade betwixt Ebbie Hopewell's house and barn.

"Grover, let me explain," Ebbie said. He came to meet me as I entered the gate. "I couldn't get word to you yesterday. Brother Jonah Higginbotham and his disciples are here. We've been in conclave and are going to have a twenty-five-year inspection of Pa and Ma's house this morning."

"But your father and mother, Ebbie," I started to say.

"Yes, they're in their graves, Grover," he interrupted, "but Ma will rise 975 years from now. She will enter that house right over there!"

He pointed to the brick house on his farm where his parents used to live. Ebbie had inherited the farm at his father's death and since that time I knew their old home had been closed; doors had been locked and shutters had

[145]

been closed over the windows. I had heard many people had tried to rent the house. But I had thought the reason Ebbie hadn't rented it was because the house in which he grew up was too close to his own house and, then, he might have sentimental reasons about not wanting to rent to strangers. I didn't know that it was the faith of his people that kept him from renting the house. I had walked past and I had driven by, over the narrow winding-lane road, many times. And in winter the old Hopewell house looked lonely standing with shutters pulled and the doors locked and with only a few snowbirds alighting in the barren branches of the initial-scarred gray-barked trees in the spacious lawn. In summer, when I passed, it was different, and Ebbie kept the lawn mowed neatly, the hedge trimmed; the tree tops were rustling clouds of green where the wild birds nested, raised their young, and filled the air with song. Ebbie's old home place was a much nicer place to live than the flimsy frame house where he lived now. Here the weather-boarding needed a new coat of paint. The roof had been patched. Birds had made round holes in the eaves where they flew in to feed their young.

"You know my word has always been good, Grover," he said. "We have always been good neighbors and this is the first time I have failed to fulfill a promise I've made you. But Brother Jonah Higginbotham and Disciples Dan Murdock, Ezekiel Burns, Travis Whittmore, Logan Marshall, Heman Wells, and Bud Adams spent the night with us. We had a crowd here last night, Grover. We put Brother Jonah in a bed by himself and two disciples in each of our other three beds. Murtie and me and the youngins slept on pallets on the floor. We've had an awful time, Grover," he continued in a low voice as we walked toward the group of elderly men. "And I just couldn't get away or send word."

My neighbor, Ebbie Hopewell, talked faster than the July wind that was bending the young green corn over the valley. Ebbie's farm lay between Big River and the foothills. And the foothills rose up to higher hills and still higher hills called mountains. The wind hummed lazy monotonous sounds. And Ebbie spoke hurried words that were filled with meaning. He was excited because on this day they would open his father's and mother's old home to see that everything was kept in order for their return to this world after a thousand years of sleep in their graves. There was a question I wanted to ask Ebbie but I didn't have time since we were walking toward Brother Jonah and the disciples. I wanted to ask Ebbie how he knew if his father and mother, who had died almost a year apart, would return together or if his mother would return first, since she died first, and if his father would return a year later. And if his mother came back to the house alone after 975 years, who would be around to meet and greet her? Ebbie, Murtie, and their children who were of the same faith would be sleeping their thousand years on Knob Hill and there might not be any relatives around. There would be no one here to welcome Ebbie's mother back home. She would arise from the grave at the age she entered and she would be old and frail. These questions bothered me the same as my hay's not being baled with a rain due here tonight. I even thought of asking Ebbie to rent his baler to me so I could bale my own hay. Ebbie had baled my hay for twelve years now. I didn't have enough hay to pay me to own a baler. It was better to pay to have it baled.

"Brother Jonah, I want you to meet my friend and neighbor, Grover Boggs," Ebbie said.

Brother Jonah was a large man, tall, slightly stooped with a skinny hand covered with rivers and tributaries of blue veins flowing under an earth-colored leathery skin. He wore little glasses in bright-wire frames. His big, dimming eyes could see over and around his glasses if they didn't focus right on the glass. He wore a white shirt, ribbon tie, a black wrinkled suit, and a black broadbrimmed flat hat that was half the size of an umbrella.

"Grover Boggs, I'm glad to know one of Brother Ebbie's friends," he spoke in a shaky voice. And then he turned to Ebbie and said, "Is Mr. Boggs a man of our faith?"

"No, but he's a boyhood friend, a good man, and a good neighbor, and he used to come and stay with me when we were boys together," Ebbie said. "He's sat with his feet under the table right over there in Pa and Ma's house many a time and et grub Ma prepared for us."

"Maybe he'd like to return when we open the doors in a few minutes," Brother Jonah said. "We don't usually let people who are not of the Faith enter the waiting homes of our departed loved ones but in this situation it will be permissible if you want to go, Mr. Boggs."

"Yes, I hadn't thought of this when I drove over," I said, "but I'll be glad to go."

I didn't know what else to say. I didn't want to refuse and maybe hurt my friend Ebbie's feelings and maybe not get my hay baled at all. I thought, maybe, if I hung around a while after they had inspected the house, Brother Jonah and his disciples would leave after lunch and Ebbie could bale my hay in the afternoon and evening. I didn't care about going back to a house that had been closed for twenty-five years.

"Now, I want you to meet my disciples," Brother Jonah said.

Then, he introduced me to Dan Murdock, who was a big man with shaven round face and deep-set eyes. Ezekiel Burns was short, fat, with a chubby face and long beard. Travis Whittmore was tall, stooped, and rawboned with big hands and a long beard. Logan Marshall was big, square-shouldered, with a bull neck and a shaven face. Heman Wells was pudgy, his blue eyes twinkled, and his voice was soft. His gray-streaked sandy-colored hair was long and his beard was red. Bud Adams was small, straight, with long hair over his shoulders and a scattered beard over his face. Each disciple was dressed in black and wore a white shirt and black umbrella hat with the broadbrim.

"Now, we will proceed with our duty to inspect the home of Brother Harry and Sister Millie Hopewell," Brother Jonah said. "Follow me."

Brother Jonah walked in front with Ebbie beside him. Ebbie carried a ring of keys that rattled in the lazy July wind. Murtie was only a step behind Ebbie, and I followed. I walked with the disciples. Murtie and Ebbie's four youngest children remained at the house. Five had married and left home. Maybe there was some reason they didn't go, I thought. Maybe they don't want to think of their dead grandparents. Maybe, too, they are too young to remember them. Along the footpath the wind bent down the grass. Then the wind would pass over and the grass would rise again. "Brethren, we are like the grass," Brother Jonah said. "But we will be like the grass for only a thousand years until our Dear Lord returns and establishes His Kingdom on earth."

"Amen, Brother Jonah," said Disciple Burns. He waddled slowly along the path on his short legs. "I say 'Amen' again, Brother Jonah. We are like the grass for one thousand years."

Stretching away toward the foothills was Ebbie's fifty acres of corn, now waist-high, clean of weeds, and freshly furrowed. His vast field of corn spread over the bottom like a green rustling cloud. And beside this cornfield was a field of similar size where the wheat had ripened to golden brown. It was almost ready for harvest. Here was a golden cloud beside the green cloud spread over the earth where the Hopewells had lived and had farmed for generations. The Hopewells were among the first people to settle our land and now, when they had died, they expected the grave to hold them for only a thousand years and they would then return to this land. And I wondered, as I walked with the disciples, about Murtie and Ebbie, my neighbors from childhood, how much difference beliefs could make among people. I was going along with them to see the house but this was only by accident. I couldn't go along with them in their beliefs, which was not the faith of their great-grandparents and their antecedents before their great-grandparents, now sleeping in unmarked pioneer graves somewhere upon this land, maybe under the earth where we were walking. No one knew. Not even Ebbie. And I wondered if all of Ebbie's and Murtie's people who had not accepted this present faith to which they held, if they were considered lost spirits among the damned. Strange thoughts went through my head as I walked toward that old brick house I had known as long as I could remember.

When we arrived at the door, Ebbie used a key in the padlock. After twisting and turning, the lock came open. It was a lock that was red with rust. Then he put a long key into the doorlock. It turned easily as if there were no lock at all. Then he pushed on the door. It didn't open easily until he put his shoulder against it and pushed, and then the door flew wide open.

"All right, Brother Jonah," Ebbie said, "there must be light. So I will open the front window shutters and lift the blinds."

Ebbie stepped inside, walking in the shaft of light that streamed through the open door which was in the path of the morning sun. He unfastened the shutter and pulled it aside. Then he threw up the blind. "Wait, Brother Jonah, until I raise the other one," he said. "Then there will be light in this part of the house." And we stood waiting until Ebbie opened another shutter and raised the blind. "All right, come in, Brethren," Ebbie said. "There is light now. See, it's just like it was the day we closed it. And that was the day we laid Pap in his temporary home on Knob Hill. That big rocker right over there was Pap's favorite chair. And this old boot-rocker was where Ma sat!"

Ebbie was deeply touched to look inside his old home again. He pulled a red bandanna from his hip pocket and wiped the tear-filled eyes.

"Yes, Brother Ebbie, I know this brings back memories," Brother Jonah said. "It's the first inspection that brings the memories. Now, when one generation fades away and an-other comes along, it is not as close to those taking their temporary rest as the first generation removed. Brother, I have given the twenty-five-year, fifty-year, and seventy-five-year inspection and I know! Ah, in the thousand years we are as the grass, the wheat, corn, and flowers!"

There was the wide, open fireplace in this room. A whisk

broom was hanging beside the fireplace to sweep up the dust. There was a basket setting there filled with wood and kindling to start a fire. There were family portraits of distant ancestors hanging on the walls. One prominent picture was of a woman with her hair combed back over her head, her hair filled with combs, and of a man beside her wearing a high stiff collar with a necktie wrapped around the collar. They didn't look like anybody I'd ever seen before.

"It is a nice home to return to," Brother Jonah said. "This place will be nice in the Paradise Kingdom. Brother Harry and Sister Millie will be proud of this place."

The air in this room was stifling for me to breathe. Air couldn't spoil like fruit in a jar, but if air could have spoiled in a closed room I would say that we were breathing spoiled air. I was still sorry I had come to this forlorn place. The air smelled of death and the room looked old-fashioned and outdated. This wasn't a cheerful place and I didn't see how anyone would want to return to it, not Millie and Harry Hopewell, or anyone else who had ever lived here. This place made me feel like I used to feel when I was a boy and had to walk past Knob Hill Graveyard in the night when I walked alone.

"Biff-buzz," was the little sound and Disciple Burns slapped his wrinkled forehead with his fat hand. "I'm stung," he said in a high voice. "I'm stung right between the eyes!"

"What stung you?" Brother Jonah asked.

"There it is on the floor," he said. "I killed whatever it was!"

"It's a hornet," I said. "Look out for a nest! Stand still. Don't anybody move!"

[152]

"Over there it is," Ebbie said. "Stand still. Stand still is right! Don't anybody move until I ease out very quietly and go over to the house and get the bee smoker. How did hornets ever get in here?"

"I wonder," Murt whispered.

The hornets' nest was larger than Brother Jonah's hat and it was fastened up in the corner where the wall met the ceiling. The black-bodied hornets with white dots on their breasts were going and coming unmindful now that we stood below them making little half-sounds when we breathed. Ebbie had tiptoed out at the door and was on his way to get the bee smoker. When he returned he came puffing ragsmoke from the smoker. And now he walked bravely over with clouds of smelly smoke before him. He sent up clouds of sickening ragsmoke around the hornets' nest. They couldn't stand the smoke. They fell to the floor by the dozens.

"Murtie, go over and get the whisk broom where Ma always kept it," Ebbie said. "Sweep these infernal things out at the front door before somebody else gets stung."

"Don't anybody get one of them stings," Disciple Burns said. "It is so painful, I am about to get sick. I may have to go outside for fresh air."

"And this smoke is unpleasant," Brother Jonah said. "Maybe we'd better all go out into the fresh air until Ebbie smokes the hornets to death and Murtie sweeps them out at the door."

Then we followed Brother Jonah outside into the bright sun-filtered July air—air from the golden wheat and growing corn, air that bent the grass and passed over and let the grass rise. It was so good to breathe. Lungs cannot taste

[153]

but I believe my lungs tasted that air because it was so good. I stood on my toes and breathed deeply and then I rocked down on my heels and exhaled. I tiptoed and breathed again as Murtie swept the dead hornets out the front door. "Oh, I feel so much better," Disciple Burns said. "Did that sting in the center of my forehead leave a place?" he asked me.

"A red pumpknot as large as a quail's egg," I replied.

"That hornet hit me so hard it nearly knocked me down," he said. "And when it hit me it popped its stiff stinger into the skull bone of my forehead with all the force it had! Ah, it was something. Were you ever stung by a hornet?"

"Yes, I've been stung by hornets," I said. "I know what you are talking about."

After Ebbie had smoked the hornets to death and Murtie had swept them out the front door, we waited for some of the smoke to thin before we went back. The air in this room, now flavored with ragsmoke, was better than the stagnant air had been to breathe. Ragsmoke-scented air is not spoiled air. Ragsmoke-flavored air is tart to breathe, and then one is sure, if he breathes it, that his lungs can taste.

Now we went into the house again and beyond this living room the house was dark.

"Maybe I'd better go to the house and fetch the lantern so I can see to open more shutters and raise more blinds," Ebbie said. "If I go into that dark I might run into another hornets' nest."

"Yes, or something else, Ebbie," I said.

Then Ebbie left the house again. And in a few minutes he returned with a lighted lantern.

[154]

"I know this house better than I know my own," he said. "I was born and grew to manhood here. And that's the only hornets' nest I've ever seen in this house."

"But in twenty-five years, Ebbie, they've found a way to get in," Disciple Burns said as he rubbed the knot on his forehead.

"You stay here until I go into the bedrooms, kitchen, and dining room and open the shutters and raise the blinds," Ebbie said.

Ebbie was gone a few minutes while we stood waiting. We heard the creaking hinges and stiff rustle of window blinds. Then he came running, swinging the lantern and shouting, "Get it loose!"

"Get what loose?" Brother Jonah said.

"Hanging to my pant leg," he said.

"It's a copperhead," Brother Jonah said. "I'd know one if I'd see it in Halifax!"

"Did it fang your leg?" Murtie asked.

"No, no, but almost," he panted. "If I hadn't jumped it would have got me. Its fangs are hung in my pant leg. I don't want the skin of my leg to touch its fangs. Stomp it. Hit it with a chair! Do something!"

"Give me the whisk broom, Murtie," I said.

"It's where Pap and Ma Hopewell used to hang it," she said. "Over the fireplace!"

I ran and got the whisk broom. "It's not big enough," I said. "Wait until I get a chair."

The short, strong, copper-colored snake was trying to get its fangs loose. There was a shovel by the fireplace. So I ran back and got the shovel.

"Don't move, Ebbie," I said. "I'll get him."

When I came down with that heavy old antiquated fire shovel's sharp edge, I cut the copperhead in two but its head was still fastened to Ebbie's pant leg. Its long-hooked fangs were securely fastened.

"All right, just a minute," I said.

Brother Jonah stood there like a statue and his disciples looked like they were ready to run. They were shaking with fear when they saw two-thirds of the copperhead squirming on the floor and a little red pool of blood. The snake's head and first third of its body was trembling, too, as the blood dripped down and splattered on the floor. I reached down with my hand and squeezed the dying copperhead's neck until its mouth opened wider; I lifted it up until its hooked fangs let loose of his pant leg.

"I'm glad you came over here with us, Grover," Ebbie said. "You know how to kill a copperhead!"

"Look at its fangs," I said. "They look like bone fishhooks!"

"Pizened things," Ebbie said.

"Are there more copperheads back there?" Brother Jonah asked.

"Yes, where there's one there are others," I said. "Ebbie and I live here in this copperhead country and we know the danger of this deadly snake."

I was almost afraid to throw the one-third of the severed snake on the floor for fear it still had enough life to reach up and bite me. But I let my grip go quickly and threw it on the floor.

"This house ain't safe for Pap and Ma," Ebbie said. "Brother Jonah, I'm glad we've entered for inspection. That copperhead was under the bed in the far bedroom."

"We'd better check and see if there are more," I said.

When I said this Disciple Burns made for the front door. Disciples Murdock, Whittmore, and Marshall followed him.

"You saved me, Grover," Ebbie said. "You're a practical man."

"We'd better have a hoe," I said.

"Go back behind the house to Pa's tool shed and you'll find a hoe," he said. "We've left his tool shed just the way he left it so when he gets back . . ."

"Reckon the handle will be strong enough," I said. "I believe we're going to have a snake fight. I know there are more copperheads and the only good copperhead is a dead one."

"Wonder how they got in here," Brother Jonah said.

"Just leave it to the copperheads," Ebbie said. "They'll find a way. And they like to get into old sunken graves, too."

I ran out of the house and went around over the well-mowed lawn to the tool shed. It wasn't locked. I opened the door and got a one-eyed chop hoe with a big hickory handle. If a hickory handle is kept dry it will be good for a few centuries. I rushed back into the house. "Come with the lantern, Ebbie," I said.

When we went back into that bedroom, there was a whole litter of young copperheads crawling around over the floor and one was up in the bed.

"You just stirred them up, Ebbie," I said. "They're out here playing a game. These copperheads are chasing each other's tails!"

When I got a fair lick, I cut down, and off went the copperhead's head close up to his skull so there wouldn't be enough of his body left to give biting power to his jaws. One lick to a copperhead and I killed twelve. It took two licks to kill the thirteenth snake for it was an old one. Then I killed four more young ones.

"They've nested and birthed in here," Ebbie said. "I'll shake the quilt and get this one out of the bed so you can use the hoe on him."

When Ebbie shook the quilt the copperhead coiled and struck, leaping twice its length. Ebbie jumped and jerked his hand back. The copperhead leaped onto the floor. And I came down just as he hit the floor and his little golden head flew in one direction while his brown-copper body squirmed on the floor and left its tablespoon of copperhead blood.

"This is awful, ain't it, Grover," Ebbie said.

"Yes, you'd better raise the quilts and sheets on the bed," I said.

When Ebbie pulled up a homemade star-quilt, he said: "I remember when Ma made this quilt." Then he lifted two blankets down to a sheet and here was a nest of copperheads not much bigger around than lead pencils. I started hitting them in the bed with the hoe. "Only a dead copperhead is a good one," I said. I killed six small copperheads lying in this bed asleep.

"What if your mother had come to this house alone and got in this bed?" I said.

"She's have gone right back to Knob Hill Graveyard," he said. "She wouldn't have been herself in blood, bone, and flesh in her natural body more than time enough for her to have died again, been laid out for burial and the funeral and the digging of the grave, planting her for another thousand years ... Ah, 'tis something!"

Well, we had killed twenty-four copperheads in this room. The second bedroom didn't have any but it had a wasps' nest and one stung Ebbie on the hand. I knocked the nest down with the hoe and Ebbie stomped it before more wasps could get out of their cells. "You can go tell Murtie to bring Brother Jonah and the disciples," I said. "These bedrooms are safe now. We'll go to the kitchen and the dining room."

While Ebbie went out to tell them to come now, I heard him say: "Bring the ash bucket to put the dead snakes in and bring the shovel to shovel them with."

When Ebbie and I were in the kitchen standing by the old wood stove, I saw a timid little mouse run from the grate. I wondered why the copperheads hadn't got him. Here were pots and pans hanging on the wall. Here was a stove, woodbox, an old-fashioned water bucket set on a little table, a wash pan, a hand towel on a roller, and a bar of soap dried in a blue dish.

"Just the way we left it the day we hauled Pap to Knob Hill," Ebbie said.

"Oh, no, Ebbie," I said. "Look, laying up there on the shelf where your mother used to put her jars." There were a few jars up there now, and there was an old coffee mill. "You didn't leave that up there, did you?"

"What kind of snake is that?" Ebbie said. "Gee, that's a big one."

"Don't worry about him," I said. "He's a gentle old house snake that got in here to get him a mouse or a bird."

"But get him down, Grover," Ebbie said.

I punched him with the end of the hoe handle and he fell off onto the floor. Well, I put my hoe down on his head gentle, not enough to hurt him, and I reached down and got him by the neck.

"I'm not going to kill him," I said. "I'm going to carry him out and turn him loose."

When I picked him up he was as long as I was tall. I went out holding him up in front of me, and he was squirming, his tail hitting the floor. When I got to the front door where four disciples stood breathing the fresh air and looking out at the pleasant valley of wheat, corn, and grass, they saw me, and got out of my way. They were shaking more than the grass. They didn't say anything and I didn't either. I walked out and put the gentle old house snake on the grass and let him crawl away. Then I went back where Ebbie was looking over the kitchen where his father and mother used to sit at breakfast time with their nine children around them.

"Ah, it brings back memories," Ebbie said. "Five up on Knob Hill with Pa and Ma taking their temporary rest, Sam in Cleveland, Ohio, Dave in San Francisco, and Bert down in Dallas. I'm the only one here! But there was once life in this kitchen. We et in the dining room only when we had company and this was every Sunday! Many good meals I've eaten at this table!"

Ebbie walked out of the kitchen slowly. The dining room was much larger and there was a white tablecloth spread over the table; plates, knives, forks, and spoons were placed there for Harry and Millie Hopewell and their nine children. "Right over there was my place," Ebbie said, pointing. "I've et many a time there."

While Ebbie was talking, I was looking around the walls and overhead. I wondered what we would find in here. Well, the chairs were placed around the table. And there were two large cupboards with glass doors, and behind these glass doors there were many kinds of dishes. Ebbie pulled out a drawer and it was filled with silver, knives, forks, and spoons. Behind us came Brother Jonah, Murtie, and the disciples Heman Wells and Bud Adams.

"This dining room is in the best shape of any room," Ebbie said.

"Yes, it's nice," I said.

There was a door leading back into the front room and I followed Ebbie through the door. The other four disciples were standing by the door. They were not following Brother Jonah on his inspection tour. Maybe the copperheads scared them, I thought. Maybe they're not too anxious for that thousand years of temporary rest. And if a copperhead got the right strike at one, it might have given him temporary rest before he was ready for it.

"This will be the hardest thing to do," Ebbie said. "See, we put Ma and Pap's clothes right here in this closet. They'll know right where to go to get them when they return. But I remember the clothes they wore and this will bring the saddest memory."

When Ebbie opened the clothespress door, two gray squirrels ran out and across the front room, climbed the wall, and went out at a hole above the window. I walked over and looked at the hole. "Squirrels have gnawed that hole so they could come in," I said. "I'll bet they've denned here in winter."

Ebbie walked into the press with his lantern.

[161]

"They've cut Pap's suits all to pieces," he said. "Here's a nest and it's still warm where they were lying asleep when I opened that door. It's right in the seat of Pap's best suit. He'll never be able to wear that suit again!"

Ebbie's eyes were moist again and he pulled the red bandanna from his pocket to absorb the tears. "They've ruined Ma's dresses, too. They've cut her coat to pieces. And it's only been twenty-five years for Ma and twenty-three for Pa."

Ebbie stepped back and closed the press door. "There will have to be some work done here," he said. "They will have to have their clothes. I'll have to fasten the squirrels out of here."

"And the snakes and the hornets," I said.

I was still carrying my one-eyed chopping hoe through the house with me. My father had always said it was bad luck to take a hoe into a house but today I thought it had been good luck that I had it with me. Murtie and Brother Jonah and Disciples Wells and Adams had made the rounds and they were standing in the living room.

"Since I'm not as young as the rest of you, I believe I will sit down a minute," Brother Jonah said. "I'll sit down in Brother Harry's favorite chair."

Brother Jonah dropped down like he was a very tired man.

"When I opened the press doors two gray squirrels ran out," Ebbie said. "I didn't know a squirrel could be so destructive. They've riddled Pa and Ma's clothes. There's not a suit for my father or a dress for my mother to wear in that press."

"Then get them new suits and dresses and hang them there and be ready for the time when they rejoicingly return from the long night of temporary sleep, Brother Hopewell," Brother Jonah said.

Brother Jonah squirmed in his chair. He seemed to be a little uneasy sitting in Ebbie's father's favorite chair.

"I'll go upstairs and open the door and just look inside the four rooms there," Ebbie said.

"Reckon you'll need me?" I asked him.

"No, I'll just look in," he said. "There has to be a closer inspection of this house and clothing replaced and repairs made."

"Amen, Brother," said Disciple Burns, who was standing over by the door.

Ebbie went up the steps and opened the door and the sound was like a November wind blowing dead leaves from the trees. The bats came down like a flock of wind-driven leaves in autumn. Brother Jonah hid his face in his arms as he squirmed in his chair. The bats flew out at the door and the Disciples Wells and Adams, who had followed through, now left the house. Murtie left with them. Ebbie ran down the steps swinging his lantern. "A thousand years is a long time," he said. "I'll have to go over this house room by room. I'm sorry, Brother Jonah."

"Say, am I feeling something in this chair?" Brother Jonah asked as he got up.

"Yes, the bottom is moving," Ebbie said. "And there's a hole in the leather seat."

"I'll say you felt something," I said. "Stand back!"

There was the big blunt copper-colored head stuck through the hole. He was looking us over with lidless eyes. His forked tongue was out of his mouth. I raised my hoe. The copperhead kept crawling out. I let him come. He was the biggest copperhead of all. And when he fell from the chair to the floor, I severed his head from his body with my hoe. "Another snake for the ash bucket," I said.

"And to think I sat down on that dangerous thing," said Brother Jonah. His voice trembled until he could hardly speak.

"Yes, Brother Ebbie, you'll have to go over this house room by room and inspect every piece of furniture," Brother Jonah said. "Wouldn't it have been awful for your dear old mother or your respected father to have returned here today?"

Now we were following Brother Jonah from the house. When we walked out into the front yard we were joined by the disciples. Murtie came with the last dead copperhead in the ash bucket. She walked out and tossed it from the bucket over the bank. "So pretty here," Brother Jonah said. "Cornfields, wheatfields, and grass! Ah, what a Paradise it is here. And a thousand years . . ."

I looked at my watch. We had had a fast inspection because we didn't linger in the house. It was only eleven now. Maybe Ebbie will get to bale my hay, I thought, as Ebbie pulled the front door shut. But he didn't lock the padlock or the door. "I've got work to do in there," he said.

As we followed Brother Jonah and Ebbie back along the path, the lazy July wind bent down the grass; after it passed over, the grass rose up again. And when the July wind blew over the green cloud of rustling corn, corn blades tried to speak to us to tell us what had been and what would be, or just whispered their secrets to each other. And when the wind blew through the ripened wheat, I thought there must be an invisible hand pulling a long invisible comb through the golden hair of the wheat.

Poems

Dawn

O Gods of Storm, beat savage-white and cold!
Crumble the ancient hills with lightning splits!
O Gods of Storm, you mighty Gods of old,
Shiver the spurging rocks to tiny bits!
Clouds, kiss the jutted land with watery kiss!
This is the time for storm; make earth awaken!
There is no better time for storm than this.
O Gods of Storm, do all you've undertaken,
Awake reptiles, cold-blooded in their sleep;
Awaken the slimy lizards, water dogs!
Awake the terrapins from mud knee-deep!
Awake the turtles and white-throated frogs!
Above all, wake the sleeping flower and tree,
Tell them it's spring and not eternity!

Give trees, you ancient Gods, new blood for veins;
Give flowers, you ancient Gods, new blood for stems;
Give snakes, you ancient Gods, new oak-leaf stains;
Give man, you ancient Gods, new sap for dreams.
Give man a new land with the high clean sky;
Give him a clean air where no factories burn;
Give man to breathe the clean wind blowing by
For lonesome waters and dew-dripping fern.
Give man green velvet earth and light green wind;
Give man the world where he can own his heart,
And own his brains and breathe no smoke-dyed wind;
New earth where he can play the different part.

· Dawn of Remembered Spring ·

Give man the spring that heavy thunders wrought;
The wine-green wind for lungs; sweet earth for thought.

O Sun of gold, ride up with golden light
And pour your golden rays on the green earth,
And make new days of all that once was night,
After that white rain baptized for new birth.
O mighty Sun, give warmth to man and flower!
Give warmth to weed, to dirt, to terrapin!
This is the new time of the newer hour,
This twilight-dawn new spring has ushered in.
Draw living forms toward you, mighty Sun!
Draw spring tendrils to you, O mighty Light!
Draw human eyes toward you, glorious Sun,
Let them look heavenward for endless light!
O Sun, eternity has come undone
In floods, O mighty Sun, of golden light!

Sing out, you mighty organs of the wind!
Bend to these blowing winds, you living trees!
Sing out, sing out, you organs of the wind,
Sing out in vast eternal harmonies.
The ancient gods are close to hear your singing;
They love the sweet clean music of the spring,
They are not deaf to winds and waters singing,
They are not blind to dawn of early spring.
What is this life without spring song and flower?
What is this world without the harmonies
Of wind and tree and flower and silver hour?
Sing out, wind-organs, in green seas of leaves;
Sing out, because this is the time to sing!
Sing out, this is the dawn, this is the spring!

You mountain rivers running to the sea
Under green mansions of the wind-stirred leaves,

[168]

· Dawn ·

Sing to the world your little symphony,
Sing to the lonesome wind, sing to the leaves.
There may be no one near to hear your singing,
Only the ancient gods in wind and leaves;
These gods are all you need to hear your singing,
You wind and leaves in mighty harmonies!
You mountain waters jumping rocks and roots,
Sing out, sing out, you lonesome waters, sing!
Sing to the drooping fern, the tendril shoots;
Sing to the bright clean wind, for this is spring.
Sing out, you mountain waters, to the sea;
Sing out your music; sing a symphony!

You scorpion, color of the red oak bark,
With belly color of white floating cloud,
Lie there and listen on your bed of bark,
Lie there and listen to wind piping loud.
Do you know pretty spring songs of the wind?
And can you tell a water symphony?
Do you love rain drumbeats or violins,
Or love a reed flute in the symphony?
What do you love, white-bellied scorpion?
You lie alive in scorpion-colored bark.
Is this spring world your sweet oblivion,
This your eternity, this night green-dark?
What do you think of these strange ancient gods
Riding on winds, hiding in gum-leaf pods?

The Poet Speaks to Cold-Blooded Snake

Cold-blooded snake, why did the thunder wake you?
Cold-blooded snake, why did you get rebirth?
Cold-blooded snake, why did creation make you
And put you down so close against the earth?
You writhe in wet leaves with red amber stain
That colors your white belly red-stain-color;
You writhe, wet limber stick, in white spring rain
And green grass carpet where the beetles smother.
You writhing copperhead, upon this carpet,
With sweet wine-colored wind so good to breathe—
Amid the fragile grass and winds that harp it,
This is spring's palace where you choose to writhe.
Cold-blooded snake, your last year's blood is frozen;
Like sap in trees your warm new blood is oozing.

The Poet Speaks to
Living Things

You living things that run, you things that crawl,
This is your life to live; this is your day.
Music is yours, the wet leaves and the clay.
Spring is your season, summer, too, and fall.
Gather your life as spring clouds gather fleece;
Gather your life as greenbriars gather wool—
Live life, you living things, in white-rain peace;
Gather your life so springtime beautiful.
All blood runs warm in spring when life awakens
New blood to flowers in juice, to trees in sap;
And new blood channels down old veins forsaken,
In man, lizard, and reptile as they nap.
You living things that crawl, you things that run,
Live this spring life! Exalt, under the sun!

Bull Blacksnake Speaks
of Love and Fear

Only for Lady Snake I show affection
As side by side we slither under cover,
So close to earth it's hard to get direction
When my cold eyes are always on my lover.
I know the foul deeds of Vile Copperhead,
Who lies, like strands of rope, coiled in the grass;
I know that Copperhead will leave us dead,
Our ribs to shine like white rings in the grass!

I do not fear the tattling April Wind,
Nor do I fear fair Kathaleen and John,
Nor Grass that tries to get us in the end,
Nor fear Gray Lizard and Green Scorpion.
I fear Vile Copperhead whose body can
Strike twice his length to hit an enemy;
I know he will keep warring on our clan;
I know that either he or I must die.

In my spring paradise I'm most content
With Lady Blacksnake in the sawbriar cove,
Entwined with her until our strength is spent
On warm spring moonless nights, our nights for love.
Her new spring skin against mine in the dark,
Her hard lips pressed to mine in evil night,
Our cold blood kindles to a fiery spark
As we embrace until dawn's chilly light.

Copperhead Speaks

Among my weeds old Whirley Pratt did sneak
Upon me when I rested by a stone
Under cool wind that blew along the creek,
That filled my ears with its sad monotone.
With thick-gloved hands he caught and housed me in
A cage not fashioned for a snake's desire;
I knew I'd lose the beauty of my skin
And my wild blood would lose some of its fire . . .
Winter, I slept cold-blooded through a dream;
But thunder woke me for spring's paradise . . .
I longed to feed and recess by my stream
Before the coming "dog days" closed my eyes.
I longed to free myself of his command.
Whirley can tell you we are not so dumb
Since meatless bones are showing on his hand
Where I planted my two fangs in his thumb.

Bull Blacksnake Defends
His Race

I am a snake; if I could speak I'd say:
"Why do you call your fellow man 'a snake'
When he has wronged you in some sort of way
And nearly caused your human heart to break?
We catch our living harvests same as man,
Sly in the shifting shades of evil night;
We better snakes war Copperhead's vile clan,
Our rattling tails drum music when we fight!
We snakes go through our lives each with one lover.
After we're resurrected in the spring
From different beds, we search and find no other.
Among you is it not a different thing?
Dear fellow man with habits more to blame,
It breaks our hearts to hear you proudly take
Our names in vain to elevate your name!
Few men attain the honor of 'a snake'!"

Miss Blacksnake Speaks

Upon rain-bleached gray-barren earth I lie,
Where bitter winterish gray-booing wind
Chills my cold blood enough to blind my eyes
But fluxions of spring sun come from behind.
I shed the coat of winter that I wear,
Since Bull and I are bathing youthful in
The golden light the second springtime bears;
We leave discarded last year's wrinkled skin.
The lilting green-clouds of wind-silver spring
Is earthly heaven for a bliss-filled pair;
If snakes could sing, we would arise and sing
And spread our gay snake music everywhere.
Your winter flesh is prisoned in cocoons
While we rejoice in second paradise;
You can't see heaven through your blinded moons
And rich-loam quilts between you and the skies.

Copperhead Speaks of
Love and Enemies

I am earth's cold phlegmatic Copperhead
With venomed fangs as sharp as sawbriar jaggers;
My body's short; my head is copperish-red;
I strike an enemy so hard he staggers!
And everything that walks or crawls or flies
Is mortal enemy to our Great Clan;
I have fought fire, hail stones and wind that sighs;
I've killed a horse, cow, fox, blacksnake and man!

The rockcliff is our rendezvous for love
Since it's more secret than the briary coves;
We lie entwined in our spring hours of love
Where neither rustling weed nor briar moves.
Unlike Blacksnake's, our great spring love is over
When Lady Copperhead lays young in loam;
Unlike old Whirley Pratt, we have one lover
And secret places of the earth are home.

I love recesses by cool autumn streams
Where bullgrass is the color of my skin
And I can rest to do my warring dreams
Molested only by grass-seething wind.
The brambled mountain graveyard is my place
To hibernate before I shall go blind;
Deep in a sunken grave, I leave no trace,
Dreaming of spring within the earth's warm rind.

[176]

Blacksnake Eavesdrops the Grass

Even the gutless cowards of the race
Met winter with the dauntless men of time;
And under snow they occupy the space
As men who made the song and spun the rhyme.
The long-haired poets came, the real, the fakes,
With all philosophies of life they'd garnered;
Masters of music came and worthless rakes
And brown-armed plowboys from the golden harvest.
In life they may have walked a different walk,
But now these varied men all sleep together.
In life we know they talked a different talk,
But now all voice is done; they lie together
In silence like the snow where no wind whines
Among weed stubble and bare trumpet vines.

Bull Blacksnake Speaks
of Final Victory

When Dog Days turned his eyes to clots of phlegm
And left him writhing blindly by a stream,
My warning-brain conceived the final chance
To make a victory of this circumstance.
With blacksnake stealth, I sprang on Copperhead,
Entwined his muscled body, squeezed him dead!
Never a chance to put his fangs in me,
That trait so common in his family tree!

In cold-blooded sleep, I dream I'll be
Awakened from winter eternity
By thunder blasts to shake my shriveled skin
And by the April rain that will seep in
To wash the sand-grains from my lidless eyes.
I'll see my Lover in spring paradise.
And there beneath soft sawbriar's tendril cover,
I'll crawl to find my resurrected Lover.

Finale of the Whispering Grass

Gray Lizard won't find John and Kathaleen;
They'll sleep in peace beneath my quilt of green!
I'll know sweet dust of Kathaleen and John,
Sweet dust for my thread-roots to feed upon!

The copperheads, blacksnakes of little worth
Whose warring clans fight to control the earth,
Will know that in the end, I'll stop their war;
I'll quilt them under dust they're fighting for!

About the Author

ᴇᔆ|| Jesse Stuart is novelist, poet, short-story writer, lecturer, teacher, writer of nonfiction, and a living legend among Southern writers. Though he has traveled widely he has found no place which he would rather call home than his native Kentucky hill country, about which he has written more than thirty books. It is here, in his beloved W-Hollow, where he and his wife Naomi Deane presently live, and where he works at some of his chosen professions in between supervising planting and harvesting on his farm.

An unusually close look at his life and work was taken in a recent book about him, *Reflections of Jesse Stuart: On a Land of Many Moods,* by Dick Perry. Mr. Perry was the Stuarts' guest and recorded on tape at their home conversations with Jesse Stuart on every subject two writers could find to discuss.

SC
STU

Stuart, Jesse

Dawn of remembered
spring   *16731*

DATE			
NOV 11			